I'm Sober. Why Is Life Still Hard?

Keys to Your Unique Journey

By

Dr. Layne Linebaugh

Copyrights

ISBN-13: 978-1985844513

ISBN-10: 1985844516

Published 2018

Cover and Author photos: Chelsea Ann Walsh Photography

Chakra Image Design: Jon Criss @ www.JCP.one

Cover Design: AN Better Publishing

Dedication

I know it was hard.

You loved me all the ways, while I did the hard things.

Without you, a life unlived.

Mom, Dad, JP, and Diane—Mahalo

Advance Praise

"I love this book! Layne Linebaugh has created an invaluable resource for coping with life, which in and of itself can be traumatic. Whether or not we have ever struggled with drug or alcohol addiction, we are all recovering from something, and so this beautifully written, easy to read, navigate and understand book can be utilized by anyone wanting to learn how listening to the voices of the mind, body, and heart can heal the soul."

Karen Barryhill Barrett
Founder of 50 is the
New Thirty Podcast

"Reading this book felt like I was sitting, having tea with a close friend who was speaking directly to me. Layne gives so many practical, holistic tips that can support anyone on their sobriety journey. I have so many great additions to my own sobriety toolbox now thanks to Layne!"

Aimee Pruitt RN,
BSN, AHE, RYT-200hr

"Speaking directly to the reader and drawing upon a number of different concepts and ideas, Dr.Linebaugh creates a simple and user friendly vision for those who have yet to find a fulfilling path in abstinence."

Mark Broadhead, MD
Addiction Psychiatrist

Table of Contents

Foreword

As a Somatic Psychotherapist, Yoga Teacher and Inquiry Coach I have worked with many clients in recovery who were still struggling to form healthy relationships with themselves and others even though their addictive behaviors had stopped.

Working alongside Layne as her Coach, I have had the privilege to witness her inspiring willingness to deep dive into further recovery as well as her stunning and ongoing transformation as a human, a Coach and now an author!

This unique and straight forward book will be a supportive guide for those who have managed to gain sobriety by stopping their addictive behaviors, only to find themselves acting out and struggling in unhealthy ways in other areas of their lives. Layne speaks in her own authentic voice as she weaves in parts of her sobriety and wellness journey along with the journeys of those who have dared to go deeper into recovery and re-discovery of their truest selves. She will give you practical tools and exercises to work with your mind, emotions and body along with an understanding of the chakra system that can further reveal the healing power of yoga.

Layne is the real deal, a woman who walks her talk and a true Sobriety Warrior.

Jodi Krahn MC, RCC

Somatic Psychotherapist, Life Coach, Inquiry Yoga

Teacher and the founder of GatherHer.

British Columbia, Canada

Introduction

I never set out to become an alcoholic or a drug addict, nor to grapple with eating disorders, struggle with money, or not know what to do in intimate relationships. Most people wouldn't wish this on themselves or anyone else. And yet, it happened. It happened to me. It's happening in every city, small town, bungalow, and ditch in the world. We cannot turn a blind eye anymore, thinking that it's getting better and that it doesn't affect each one of us—because it does affect us, *all* of us. One person may act out an addiction pattern, which affects the whole family, and we are all addicted or recovering from something. We don't want to admit that our disconnection from ourselves, the earth, our spiritual selves, and each other have perpetuated a planet of addiction.

Since at least 1935, when Bill Wilson and Dr. Bob Smith founded Alcoholics Anonymous, there has been hope for people who find themselves in the horror of an addiction story. The Anonymous programs have been a savior for humanity, a light in the dark that beforehand contained hospitals, institutions, and death as the only options for healing. These programs work, but the percentage of those it works for is still alarmingly low. Only one in four addicts will get and stay sober through the method of twelve-step programs.

It's not enough. The creation of opiate medications has changed the landscape of addiction, and it isn't pretty. Humanity is bombarded with technology, available all day and night—and our collective psyche, so adaptable and evolved, is struggling with gambling, social media, sugar, disordered eating, violent thinking, power addictions, and war addictions. The list goes on, and the solutions remain weak in comparison to what they are up against.

But there is hope. There are solutions. There are pioneers on the forefront of solving our disconnection, trauma, and addiction epidemic. These people—such as Tommy Rosen, Noah Levine, Dr. Gabor Maté, and Johann Hari—are forging ahead with or without the methods of traditional twelve-step programs and looking deeper into what exactly happens when humans become addicted and why.

Please understand me. I believe in the power of the twelve steps. Those steps are *good*. Those programs *work*. They just don't work for everybody, all of the time at the same time. I don't feel that they were meant to be the last words and the only help for addiction. I do feel that they are and can be brilliantly supplemented with new depths of learning and understanding.

Consider the following questions:

- Are you looking for more out of your sobriety?

- Are you still overwhelmed with problems you thought sobriety was supposed to fix?

- Do you feel out of control with new addictions and issues?

- Are you feeling angry, sad, anxious, and fearful much of the time?

- Are you in pain? Or depressed?

- Are your relationships fraught with misunderstandings?

- Are you still struggling with finances and finding meaningful work?

- Are you grappling with one or all of these problems and people keep telling you to pray or "think positive" and you've worked the steps (maybe more than once) and you have done all the "right" things and you still feel like a hot mess?

- Do you know, deep down, that you didn't get sober to just have more problems you don't understand?

- Are you thinking, "Is this really all there is? I didn't sign up for a 'nice, little life.'"

- Do you know that you are here for more?

- Do you feel you have a purpose, a flame that didn't go out while you were in active addiction? Why should hardships put out this flame now?

If your answers are yes, I say, "Welcome to my world." This is what life was like for me before I was introduced to the insights and practices you get to explore in the pages of this book.

I have been where you are. I was over three years sober and in emotional, mental, and physical pain. I was doing the "right" things, and they helped. They just weren't explaining the appearance of "emotional anorexia," addiction transfer, loads of physical injuries, the resurfacing of my distorted body image, as well as a host of other problems that sort of blew my mind.

Wasn't sobriety supposed to be at least a little easier than this?

Yes.

There is a way through.

Before I show you why you are sober and still having a life full of problems, I need to explain some enlightening concepts about how people with histories of trauma and addiction tend to operate. I need to explain how a person can work all the twelve-step programs in the world, enjoying solid sobriety, and can still feel unfilled and anxious. I will explain why you can't "just be happy." You will find all of this and more in the pages ahead.

This book is not one of statistics about addiction. It is not a book about meditation (although I do gently cover some breath work and meditation techniques). It is not a book about the importance of nutrition and exercise in the healing of trauma and addiction. It is not a book about any of the twelve -step programs. It is not about yoga as an answer to all of your problems.*

It *is* a book about the processes, inquiry, and learning that took me beyond facing sobriety on my own. It is a book about the practices and keys that brought me to true recovery (discovery), which I did not find solely in AA or in the twelve-steps. It is a book about how Grounding and Boundaries practice and simple chakra work, combined with these keys, can bring you a depth of self-knowledge you may have not have known was possible. These practices worked for me, and they work for my clients and colleagues. I believe they will work for you, also.

I won't lie to you. I still have a life that includes

problems, but they don't feel insurmountable anymore. Writing this book called for me to face all of the places where I was using the best of my tactics to "play small" and make excuses for myself and my behavior. Sometimes, I still play the child and don't use my own knowledge. Those times come less often and don't last as long as I have and use the tools to sort stuff out. If I'm still wallowing in some messy situation and not understanding why, then my coaches (yes, I have coaches) come along and help me unravel the mystery. They share so that I share, and I share so that you will grow and share too.

In the end, this book is for you. It's so these tools and keys will be more available to more people, because we have a mission here. Our mission is to make a giant dent in the understanding of addiction. Our mission is to end the stigma of addiction and recognize us for the hero's that we are. Our mission is to stop addiction before it ravages lives and families, and we can only do this by diving in to the deep lakes and rivers of our own personal stories. Our mission is to "grow ourselves up" on this most sacred of adventures.

*Please see the references and further reading section of this book for author and book recommendations covering these topics.

Note: As I was writing this book, I became aware that many prominent people in the field are now classifying addiction as "substance use disorder." Research shows that it is more of a mental health problem than of morality. Classifying addiction as a true disorder is a wonderful step toward ending the stigma we face. I believe in these findings, as I explain throughout the book and in the chapter on the connection between the disorder and trauma. I'm also inclined to think that the pattern in the human brain to disconnect using relationships, television, and social media, for example is the same as when one uses a substance to feel different. I chose not to change the wording of "addiction" in this book so as to keep the text and thoughts uniform.

Chapter One—Why Am I Still Struggling?

When I met Rian (pronounced Ryan), she was strong in her sobriety, but life was heavy on her soul. She was a little over three years sober and had made huge strides in her desire to become financially, emotionally, mentally, and physically sober. She was world-weary and tired.

The years of sober living, while kinder than active addiction, had been beset with loss, illness, injuries, and enormous financial difficulties. She was grappling with emotional pressure, as she had never learned about emotions and how to properly handle them.

In many ways, I was amazed she was handling life as well as she was. She really is tenacious and has a warrior spirit shining through the layers of disappointment and years of trauma that she has endured.

We spoke about her need to understand what was happening in her life. She is a smart person and rationally knows that life is not all unicorns and rainbows, yet why did she continue to have such a hard time no matter what she did?

She knew that there had to be a reason she had gotten sober.

She knew that her spirit was strong and that there

had to be an answer beyond the hardship.

This is why Rian needed me. She needed me to guide her through a deeper understanding of what was happening in her life. She had important work to do on this planet, and it wasn't "playing small" and letting life and her problems overwhelm her. She needed someone to believe in her and to help her sort through her trauma, problems, and emotions.

So I showed Rian the tools that I am going to show you—the tools that would be integral to understanding herself and her life—and how she could apply them to integrate and transmute these issues into magical, life-affirming strengths. These "problems" would become her story and part of her own unique life DNA.

During my thirty-five years of disordered eating and substance abuse, I was also a seeker of peace and happiness. I devoured spiritual texts and self-help books, attended personal growth seminars, as well as got a fancy degree with letters after my name. I meditated, prayed, was prayed over, and went on a million cleanses and diets. I attended church. I trained in Clinical Hypnotherapy, as well as Neuro-linguistic Programing. I exercised, and I'm even a part of a relay race team that travels the United States running 200-mile relays.

All of these things helped, and I give them much credit for the fact that I retained some measure of sanity when I chose a sober path. I am grateful for the belief in "something greater than myself," which kept me going during the times that I wanted to end it all.

Imagine my surprise when, after the initial period of expected difficulty in sobriety, that while now I could be consistent with all of my studies and practices, sober life was still *fuckcking hard*. Geez. This felt like my life in addiction, only now I had to feel everything and no one was giving me any satisfactory answers for my pain.

I mostly wanted to hide. My life (don't misunderstand here, it was better by far than before) consisted of work, trail running (when not injured) or walking with pups, AA meetings, and being with close friends and family.

Oh, and yoga. I would go to yoga even when I felt tired, fat, and ugly. I felt connected to myself and others in a way that I had not before experienced, during yoga practice. Yoga began to heal my distorted body image patterns. Yoga gave me friends with whom I could really be myself and express my darkest fears and flaws.

Eventually, yoga gave me the keys that you now hold in your hand. Yoga led me to the training, experiences, and practices in this book. These experiences, practices, and inspirations I will share with you. I will share my story and the stories of my clients and colleagues.

I don't want you to stand on the sidelines of your life anymore, wondering what you are missing. I have been given this wondrous gift that is not mine to keep. I want *you* to grow and expand and revel in your unique sober journey.

Before we begin, here is a short "map" of the territory we will be covering.

Grounding and Boundaries. In this foundational chapter, we will discover Grounding and Boundaries practices. In short, people who have been traumatized and addicted are classically disconnected from their roots. In many ways, they are frozen in time and running from the events that caused their disconnection in the first place. They have no concept of proper boundaries because theirs were most likely shattered. They have to "grow themselves up" in sobriety and have no ground upon which to do so. No wonder one feels powerless, lost, and alone.

A Little about Chakras. Here we will unlock the power of your body's chakra system. A chakra is a center of organization that receives, assimilates, and represents life force energy. They are of Eastern Wisdom orientation and an integral piece of your sobriety puzzle. Here we will combine this wisdom with the power of Grounding and Boundaries, and you will receive your first exercise.

Magic Key #1: Become a Thought Warrior. Here I will introduce the Four Voices and go into detail about the Mind Voice. I know it doesn't seem like it now, but I believe your addiction story and all of your problems are a gift to you, wrapped up in a really funny package. Most of humanity is walking around in a daze caused by neon lights, spiritual longing, untended addictions, and the desperate attempt to control the unknown. Unquestioned thoughts rattle our bones. People in sobriety are encouraged to mediate and not listen to their "monkey minds." They are told they have huge egos and should humble themselves, shut up and listen, look at character defects, and basically shut down the Voices that have been clamoring to be listened to for years. They have no idea how to hear the messages of their mind, emotions, body, and soul. Our minds become devoid of true beauty. We feed our bodies and our minds "food" of violence, apathy, and poor language. Sobriety wakes you up in the most painful of ways. The gift is that now you are "woke." If you choose to question your thoughts and not settle for a "nice," sober life, you are bound to rail against your problems, which become sign posts for a deeper awakening and consciousness.

Magic Key #2: Your Body *Is* the Key. Your body contains your history, your story and is the part of you that is always in the present moment. Your mind, emotions, and soul can be in the past, the present, and the future— but not your body. Learning to listen to and decipher the messages your body holds is powerful medicine. The Body Voice and messages are rarely, if ever, considered in traditional recovery programs. Welcome to being a pioneer of exploring what your body has to tell you.

Magic Key #3: Emotional Messengers. You have been taught that certain emotions are good and others are bad and that you shouldn't be overly emotional. If you are anything like the majority of people who choose a sober life, you may be grateful you can now feel emotions, while at the same time, feel completely overwhelmed by them. There are messages in your emotions you have not been told about. These messages can support you in navigating the challenges of your life. Acknowledging and befriending your emotions is powerful stuff!

Magic Key #4: The Voice of Your Soul. Your Soul

Voice is usually perceived as God, Buddha, Higher Power, Spirit, etc. It's what guided you to purchase this book. Listening to this voice takes time, space and solitude in most cases, especially in the beginning stages. It's why we do all the prayer, meditation, and yoga practices: in order to hear our Soul Voice.

I have come to believe that *not* knowing about these different voices and messages, and being told that we are defective and selfish, has the great potential to harm a person in a discovery process.

When I learned about these foundations and that I could communicate with my body, emotions, mind, and soul, I felt excited! I hope you feel the same because there is power in the pages to follow.

This book will also address some of the areas of life you have probably already noticed that are not fun and that are most likely causing you the majority of your problems. You will use Grounding and Boundaries and the keys to navigate these areas with greater ease and understanding. Relationships, money, addictions (and transference), disconnections, and overcoming the impact of trauma are the big obstacles most humans face in all the stages of recovery. Ignoring these areas can cause illness, injuries, depression, anxiety, misplaced shame and outbursts of rage, along with a host of other issues.

Addiction is noisy. Recovery is noisy and complicated. Having a life full of problems is noisy, complicated, and confusing. Connection to your inner world and listening to the messages of your Four Voices requires space, solitude, time in nature, and quiet. Many people in discovery find comfort in physical movement and exercise. It's a good solution and works, and yet it doesn't contain the whole story. Yes, we need to be grounded and in our bodies in order to listen, but we also need space and time to complete the picture. Restorative yoga slows everything down and allows you to be in your body, as well as gives you the required space and time for the answers to flow. Of course, you will also want to be able to ask the right questions. This book will teach how to do just that.

We will travel through the desert of despair, which these very human life challenges can cause. We will cross valleys and scale mountains to find the treasure chest of your unique and brilliant flame. I'm so happy you've decided to join me.

Chapter Two—Grounding and Boundaries

I cannot stress enough the importance of Grounding and Boundaries practices in addiction recovery. Turns out, these concepts and practices are also super relevant in long-term sobriety and skillful life management. This solid method is the foundation of my work with myself and all of my clients. It is the container that we can build around ourselves as we heal. This container will help you self-reference and self-resource as you move through your journey.

Disassociation and distraction may have been necessary for survival and sanity at one time, but now it's only causing problems and you need a way out. Grounding is the first step on your journey to a happier, more adult you. It is a way for you to stay present and not disconnect.

You may be wondering what grounding even means . . .

Grounding

"A connection between an electrical conductor and the Earth, grounds are used to establish a common zero-voltage reference for electric devices in order to prevent potentially dangerous voltages from arising between them and other objects." – *American Heritage Dictionary*

In direct relation to electricity, the human body (and

everything else on the planet) is made of energy and most of the same elements of earth. When we die, our bodies return to earth matter. So it makes sense that we should be connected to the earth during our life time. Earth sustains us and gives us hope, home, and grounding. Many of us are not taught that to put our feet on the ground, touch a rock, or wiggle our toes will instantly connect and calm us if we let it.

If you can, try this now. Go outside, put your feet on the earth, wiggle your toes, and breathe. If you can't do this, put both feet on the floor, hold onto something solid nearby and imagine your spirit inhabiting your body, all the way to your toes. Notice what you smell, feel, taste, and hear. This will bring you into the present moment, giving you wisdom and space to unravel your thoughts and emotions.

We can and do have roots connecting to our earth home—we just can't see them. Give this idea a chance, as it is the most important gift for your journey to a more peaceful and relaxed feeling—no matter where you are on your journey. I realize that you probably don't know me and that it may be hard to trust me at this time. I just ask that you suspend your disbelief for a moment. I do know what I am talking about.

Grounding will help you sort out your problems. It's is a simple practice you can do anywhere, anytime, and no one will even know you are doing it. It's a secret superpower you are going to love.

Boundaries

"A boundary is anything that marks a limit."—
American Heritage Dictionary

"A psychological boundary protects an individual and helps to set a realistic limit in an activity or relationship."—Psychology Dictionary

Your boundary is your personal space, and it is a part of your being. It is your personal bubble. You can feel it when you are in a crowded elevator or when people stare at you. It is your container and contains your mental, physical, emotional, and soul "bodies." You may have heard it called your aura. In neurological terms, it is your proprioceptive territory. It is the system your body uses to know "where you are in space."

Your proprioceptors map your body and your environment, so you can interact competently in the physical world. They map your home, car, tools, work space, and all of your habits.

When we can ground ourselves and focus our attention in our bodies, we'll begin to create definition in our psyches, which then allows us to firmly delineate our personal boundaries.

An easy way to imagine boundaries is to picture yourself sitting in the middle of a six-by-three-inch yoga mat. The mat is your boundary. You are sitting quietly and suddenly a group of yogis enter the room and start walking all over your mat. That doesn't feel very good does it? What if you get up in the middle of class and go sit on someone else's mat? That isn't cool either, is it?

Learning about boundaries and how to tell if yours are being crossed or if you are crossing others' is one of the most important practices to living a fulfilled and happy sober life. You will be amazed at the self-awareness that comes with setting proper, healthy boundaries.

It is important and most efficient to pair grounding work with boundaries work, since in our distracted and disassociated society most of us don't see ourselves as distinct individuals with clear boundaries. This is to the great detriment of our health in all aspects. We have a hard time focusing enough to protect or define ourselves, leaving us even more distracted and avoiding our inner lives. We are scattered and unprotected.

It's a sad fact that most humans on the planet are taught little to nothing about their basic rights, how to create safety for themselves, and how to connect to their own very earthy human nature. Instead, most of us are abused in some manner (too many, severely) by the very people we have to look to for survival and nourishment. Our parents have been mistreated and abused. In turn, they hand down legacies of abuse and disconnection. We are seeing firsthand the severe repercussions.

Many experts in the field of addiction are now agreeing that the "-isms" are all an outcome of disconnection and trauma somewhere in childhood. Obviously, physical and sexual abuses are what we think of when we discuss abuse, but there are the emotional and mental abuse cases as well. The abuse doesn't have to be severe. Bessel Van Der Kolk, M.D., the author of The Body Keeps the Score, recounts that little abuses over time can cause the same traumatic outcome as violent abuse.

Severe illnesses and accidents can also have a disconnecting effect. Fighting in the family, divorce, abandonment and poverty conditions, as well as bullying can have a detrimental effect on us when we are little people with no safety net or understanding of what is happening to us. Lack of affection, death of pets and loved ones, and being pushed too hard to measure up are more examples of circumstances that predetermine one to turn to substance abuse, acting out, gambling, sex addiction, social media distractions, endorphin addiction, co-dependency, and other ways of coping with life circumstances that are just plain painful.

All of the above are examples of boundary impairment. If you are to have a successful adventure, you must have a strong foundation (grounding) and container (boundaries) around your very human psyche.

I honestly do not know of one person with addiction patterns and their associated problems who has proper boundaries. Not one of my clients comes to me able to set boundaries or knowing how to not cross the boundaries of others. Everyone is all up in everyone else's business, causing major relationship and personal problems.

In the year that Rian and I have been working together, she has had some new enormous problems,

13

such as being asked to leave a job that was (at first glance) very important to her financial stability. This loss was rightfully a bitter pill to swallow. Yet, by using the strength of her Grounding and Boundaries, she was able to turn this event around to her advantage and move on to her true calling and purpose in life. It has still been a trying time. She had to (temporarily) restructure her budget and make room to feel and understand anger, sadness, and grief.

In the past, an event such as this would have sent her into a tailspin of despair, resentment and paralysis for months. This time she processed through and had moved on in a matter of weeks.

As Rian delves deeper into the foundation of Grounding and Boundaries, she finds greater resiliency as she firmly faces new challenges that appear.

What if addiction brings us to the threshold of destruction so that we will take more profound glances inward? What if our seemingly endless problems shake us awake so that we put on our explorer hats and go on journeys of the soul?

Chapter Three—A Little about Chakras

I knew Zena from when we both worked in restaurants, and we had done some hard partying together back in the day. After I quit drinking, I would see her from time to time and knew she was really struggling. One of the gifts of sobriety is truth-telling. I had no reason to not be public with my journey, so Zena knew I was no longer drinking.

We agreed it was a fit for us to work together and then quickly discovered Zena would need to "grow herself up." She had been the recipient of abuse and poor parenting. She had severe boundary impairment. Her stages of childhood development had been skewed, and she had no sense of what—if anything—was "normal."

She says, "It was just noise and pain and a terrible discomfort I was willing to do just about anything to escape. I wasn't able to put all of the pieces together in a way that helped me feel like a whole thing, rather than a million pieces of one. It was confusing and all I knew how to do was react. I didn't know how to see it or how to understand it. My mind-body connection wasn't just out of sync, it was lost entirely! The discomfort of my life was too much, and so I turned to things that helped to numb the pain I was feeling. I couldn't bear it, so I chose not to feel anything at all. Well then that stopped helping too and became a problem all its own. That is when I decided I needed real help. My ways quit working (well they never actually did) and my life was on a fast track to being broken forever."

This is an accurate description of a "life interrupted."

In a perfect world, we would all mature and develop just like the charts would have us believe is "normal."

More truthfully, trauma and disconnection *are* the "norm," and most of us have to re-parent ourselves when we reach adulthood. This is especially true if you have experienced trauma, disconnection, and subsequent addiction.

Fortunately, the chakra system is available to help us "grow ourselves up." Besides being an ancient and evolved practice, it contains much valuable information about the human body and psyche, as well as describes the full range of the human developmental process.

The study of the chakra system is fascinating, and I hope you dig deeper as you progress upon your journey. For our purposes here, I will give a simple description of each chakra, the basic human rights correspondences, and why they are important to you and your health. Blocked energy in our chakras can often lead to illness and difficulty, so it is important to understand what each chakra represents. A little knowledge goes a long way, and the chakra system is a beautiful way to take responsibility for your own fulfillment and to "grow yourself up" in an intelligent manner.

Note: Again, this is a simplified version and all that you will need to move through this book. If you find yourself confused, feel free to move ahead to the other chapters—just know that you will want to refer back to this information. It's good wisdom though, so give yourself the opportunity to assimilate something new. When you want to study further, the resources are found at the end of the book under Recommended Reading.

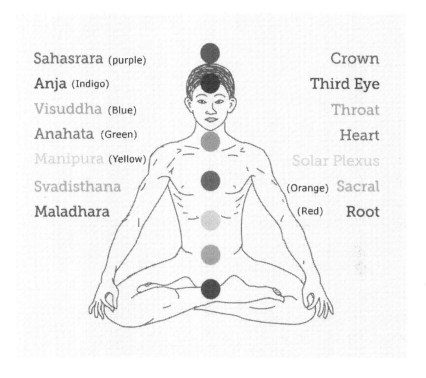

Sahasrara (purple) — Crown
Anja (Indigo) — Third Eye
Visuddha (Blue) — Throat
Anahata (Green) — Heart
Manipura (Yellow) — Solar Plexus
Svadisthana — (Orange) Sacral
Maladhara — (Red) Root

Chakras: The Wisdom of the East

"Chakra is a Sanskrit word literally meaning 'wheel.' These centers were named as such because of the circular shape to the spinning energy centers which exist in our subtle etheric body, the non-material energetic counterpart to our physical body. There are seven main chakras and

they are located along the spine extending out the front and back of the body."—William J.D. Doran

Root Chakra (Muladhara)

Located at the base of the spine, this chakra is red and associated with survival issues, such as nourishment, financial independence, security, home, family, roots, grounding, and appropriate boundaries.

Basic right: to be here and to have.

Base emotion: fear.

Traumas and Abuses include: birth trauma, abandonment, physical neglect, poor physical bonding with the mother, malnourishment and feeding difficulties, major illness and surgeries, physical abuse or violent environment, enema abuse and inherited traumas from the parent's survival fears.

Healing practices include: reconnecting with the body, physical activity, lots of touch and massage, hatha yoga, look at earliest relationship to mother, reclaim right to be here.

Sacral Chakra (Svadhistana)

Located in the lower abdomen, about two inches below the navel and two inches in, the second chakra is orange and is associated with movement, sensation, emotions, sexuality, desire, needs, and pleasure.

Basic right: to feel and have pleasure.

Base emotion: guilt.

Traumas and Abuses include: sexual abuse (covert or overt), emotional abuse, volatile situations, neglect, coldness, rejection, enmeshment, emotional manipulation, overuse of playpen, religious or moral severity, physical abuse, alcoholic families, and inherited issues from those who have not worked out their own issues around sexuality.

Healing practices include: movement therapy, emotional release or containment as appropriate, inner child work, boundary work, addiction recovery programs, assign healthy pleasures.

Solar Plexus Chakra (Manipura)

Located in the upper abdomen at the stomach area, the third chakra is bright yellow and is associated with energy, activity, autonomy, individuation, will, self-esteem, proactivity, and power.

Basic right: to act and be an individual.

Base emotions: shame and anger.

Traumas and Abuses include: shaming, authoritarianism, volatile situations, domination of will, physical abuse, enmeshment, age inappropriate responsibilities, and inherited shame from parents.

Healing practices include: grounding and emotional contact, deep relaxation, stress control, vigorous exercise, martial arts, sit-ups, build ego strength, release or contain anger, work on shame issues, strengthen the will, encourage autonomy.

Heart Chakra (Anadhata)

Located in the center of the chest just above the heart, the fourth chakra is emerald green and is associated with love, balance, self-love, relationship, intimacy, anima/animus, devotion, reaching out, and taking in.

Basic right: to love and be loved.

Base emotion: grief.

Traumas and Abuses include: rejection, abandonment, loss, shaming, constant criticism, and unacknowledged grief—including that of parental divorce, and death of loved ones, loveless, cold environments, conditional love, sexual or physical abuse, and betrayal.

Healing practices include: breathing exercises, pranayama, work with arms, reaching out, taking in, journaling, self-discovery, psychotherapy and coaching (examine assumptions about relationship, emotional release of grief, forgiveness when appropriate, inner child work, codependency work, self-acceptance, anima/animus integration).

Throat Chakra (Vissudha)

Located at the throat, the fifth chakra is bright blue and is associated with communication, creativity, listening, resonance, and finding one's own voice.

Basic right: to speak and be heard.

Base issue: lies.

Traumas and Abuses include: lies, mixed messages, verbal abuse, constant yelling, excessive criticism (blocks creativity), secrets (threats for telling), authoritarian parents (don't talk back), alcoholic or chemically-dependent family (don't talk, don't feel).

Healing practices include: loosening neck and shoulders, releasing voice, singing, chanting, toning, storytelling, journal writing, automatic writing, silence practices, non-goal-orientated therapy, psychotherapy and coaching (learn communication skills, complete communications, letter writing, inner child communications, and voice dialogue).

Third Eye Chakra (Anju)

Located at the forehead between the eyes, this chakra is indigo and is associated with image, intuition, imagination, visualization, insight, dreams and vision.

Basic right: to see.

Base issue: illusions.

Traumas and Abuses include: what you see doesn't go with what you are told, invalidation of intuition, psychic occurrences, ugly or frightening environment (war zone, violence).

Healing practices include: creation of visual art, visual stimulation, meditation, psychotherapy and coaching (coloring and drawing, art therapy, working with memory, connecting image with feeling, dream work, hypnosis, guided visualizations, past life regression therapy).

Crown Chakra (Sahasrana)

Located at the very top of the head, this chakra is violet in color and is associated with transcendence, immanence, belief systems, higher power, divinity, union and vision.

Basic right: to know and to learn.

Base issue: attachment.

Traumas and abuses include: withheld information, education that thwarts interest, forced religiosity, invalidation of one's beliefs, blind obedience (no right to think for one's self), misinformation, lies, and spiritual abuse.

Healing practices include: re-establish physical and emotional connection, re-establish spirit connection, learning and study, spiritual discipline, meditation, psychotherapy and coaching (examine belief systems, develop inner witness, and work with higher power).

Note: Healing practices for each chakra are best partnered with a professional coach or therapist.

Putting It All Together

Good job hanging in there with all this technical stuff. Now I'm going to teach you the exercise I teach all of my clients during our first session. The Grounding and Boundaries practices are yours forever, and I recommend you start your day with this visualization. Return to it often throughout the day and watch yourself calm down, be more present, and able to handle a myriad of problems with greater ease. Practice does make a difference, so do this *a lot!*

Exercise

Sit in a comfortable cross legged position or in chair with your feet flat on the floor. It's helpful if the space you are in is quiet and not too brightly lit. Bring your attention to your feet touching the floor, to how your clothes feel on your skin. Notice anywhere your body is touching something. You might tune into textures and things like temperature. Now notice any smells in the area around you. Get curious. Become more and more aware. Let your breathing deepen, taking a big inhale, letting your belly expand with the inhale and contract with the exhale. How does that feel? Just notice, don't try to change anything. Now notice what you are hearing. Maybe pick out one sound or notice all the sounds together. What do you taste? Bring your awareness to the emotions you are feeling. Where are they in your body? Now become aware of what you are seeing behind your eyelids. Maybe you see the light playing on your eyelids—maybe you "see" an image or memory with your inner sight. Just become aware of all these sensations. Continue with deep breaths in and out, letting your chest and belly rise and fall.

Bring your attention to the very base of your spine where the root chakra lives. You might even be able to see or feel the red color. Imagine sense and feel a grounding cord begin to reach down from that root chakra, through the floor, the foundation of the building, through all the layers of the earth, and into the molten core of the earth. This is your grounding cord, and you get to make it look however you want. Just imagine it strong and flexible. It can be a tree root, a cord of golden light, even a dragon's tail. Let it anchor into the center of the earth.

Now, bring your attention to the bottoms of your feet. Imagine roots growing from the bottoms of your feet down, down into the ground and into the layers of the Earth.

Begin to bring the energy from your grounding cord up to meet those roots in the bottom of your feet, and let the energy combine. Now, bring grounding earth energy into the bottoms of your feet. Make earth energy the colors of the earth—greens, golds, browns, reds, yellows—and send this energy up into your feet, ankles, calves, knees, legs, thighs, and into the pelvis to meet back up at your root chakra. Take your time with all of this. Make sure you are checking back in with your breath and all the sensations of touch, emotions, taste, sound, sight, and smell.

Notice that you feel connected and supported by the earth, the earth's energy and your grounding cord. Cool, huh?

Begin to send some of that earth energy and color sipping up the back of your spine. You will stop and say "hi" to each chakra along the way. Send that energy up into the pelvis between the hip bones, and notice the orange of the sacral chakra. You can pause here or anywhere you like, just be sure and stay with all the sensations. Following the curve of your lower back into the area right behind the V of your rib cage, notice the yellow of the solar plexus chakra, the center of your will, confidence, and "getting things done." Breathe in the power of this area. Continue up to the back of the heart, to the heart chakra with its emerald green, the center of love and emotion. Expand your breath into the heart, both front and back. Let that earth energy travel up the curve of the upper back into the throat area, into the bright blue of the throat chakra that rules communication. Now, continue up the back of the head to the area right across from the brow or third eye chakra with its indigo color. Continuing to breathe, send the stream of earth energy out the top of the head, directly through the purple of the crown chakra.

Pause here. Check in with how you feel. You cannot do this wrong, but it will take some practice, just like any other new skill.

Imagine light coming down into the top of your head, through your crown chakra. This is divine source light and can be whatever color shows up for you. Let it fill up your mind, your brain, getting into every nook and cranny. Let this light heal and massage and restore your natural energy and heal your thinking. Send divine light into your sinuses, your mouth, and jaw, filling, healing and connecting all the cells of your body with all the cells of your soul. Bring that healing source light into your neck and the tops of your shoulders, and send it down your arms into the elbows, forearms, wrists, hands, and out your fingers. Let that light make its way into the chest and lungs, reaching into and around the rib cage. Breathe it into all the structures of your lungs, the alveoli and tissues, and let that light be carried into the bloodstream to nourish and heal all the way to your toenails. Light up your liver, your heart, gall bladder, spleen, stomach, making its way into the abdominal cavity and healing all those very important organs. Heal and connect the large and small intestines, bladder, colon, and your genital area. Bring that divine source light into your pelvis to mix with that earth energy. Notice how this feels to be connected, held and supported by the earth, to be connected and healed by the divine. Just notice. Breathe this feeling in and out. It may have been a very long time, if ever, that you remember feeling this relaxed and supported.

This is grounding through the chakras.

When you are ready, let your eyes gently flutter open, keeping a soft gaze. We will now explore your personal boundary space.

Stand up with your feet placed firmly on the floor. Extend both arms straight out in front of you. This is the front of your boundary. Now extend your arms out the sides. These are the sides of your personal bubble. You can turn around and place your arms out or just draw a circle behind you. This is the back of your boundary. Now bring both arms above your head, this is the top of your boundary. Bending your knees, bring your arms to the floor and imagine the drawing of your boundary below your feet. The whole thing is sort of an egg shape with you as the yolk in the middle. It's your safe space.

Standing tall again, close your eyes and imagine the boundary around you. Now make it a bright neon color, so you can vividly see it in your mind's eye. It really is a thing. The more you work with this, the more you will be able to feel it.

Now, while you are still in this meditative state (you can sit back down), make your Boundary Bubble a safe place where you can go to restore yourself. Imagine your favorite nature setting or fluff it up with pillows, soft blankets, plants, animals, spirit guides, whatever you want to have in there to support, comfort, bring you energy and love. (It is not recommended to place people inside your safe place.)*

I invite you to return here often.

This exercise is your foundation. It is the "solid ground" upon which you will learn to stand. It is the fortress where you can feel safe, loved, and supported. It is always with you. You only need to embrace it, visualize it, and use it.

Congratulations! You now have your foundation and your fortress. Even better, you get to take them with you. How fun is that?

Are you ready to uncover the Magic Keys for solving

your sobriety problems? Let's go!

*For a free audio recording of this process, please visit my website www.LayneLinebaugh.co.

Chapter Four—Magic Key #1: Become a Thought Warrior

Melecia is a bright woman with a feisty personality. She is in her thirties and is a Special Education teacher holding a BA in Elementary Education and a Master's in Special Ed with a concentration in moderate to intense intellectual disabilities. She also provides in-home care. She loves dogs and working out, and she dreams of having a ranch for people eighteen and over who have special needs.

She began coming in for sessions after realizing she was feeling numb in her life. She had problems with overworking, overeating, and procrastinating except when she was at school or work.

As with all my new clients, she needed to learn Grounding and Boundaries work just to begin restoring her energy and trust in herself. Once she became skilled with this, we began to dig a bit deeper.

Humans are made up of exquisite pieces. We are part children and part adults. We are earth, emotions, and ideas. These parts can become fractured and hidden.

Melecia was really struggling with procrastination. She was paralyzed by thoughts of unworthiness. There was a part of her (version 1.0) so terrified of doing something wrong that she would refuse to do anything she didn't know she could do perfectly. The pain of not trying anything new was easier for her than the pain of failing, but she didn't know that. Using neurolinguistics programming tools, thought work, and images the body gave us, we were able to "talk" to another part of Mel (version 2.0) that was ready to get out there and make things happen.

Integrating pieces of the psyche like this is a fascinating process and must be undertaken gently with agreement from all parts. With gentle titration, back and forth between the two versions, they came to an agreement. Version 2.0 could go out and do all the things, perfectly or imperfectly, and version 1.0, who still did not want any part of that, would not get in the way.

In this same session, Melecia was also treated to a vision of version 3.0. She's "beautiful, fierce, confident, perfectly imperfect, and happy."

Each day and each time I am treated to seeing her, I would have to say she's well on her way to version 4.0.

Remember when I spoke about your Four Voices? You have a Mind Voice, Body Voice, Heart Voice, and a Soul Voice. These voices are the Magic Keys you will use to unlock the challenges and mysteries you have been facing on your sobriety journey.

The Mind Voice

Your Mind Voice is the one that we as humans access the most. It's the monkey mind, the one always thinking and thinking. We need it. It's a protection method, and quite frankly, we couldn't operate without it. It does have good information for you—it just gets a little crazy sometimes, and we need to give it something else to do.

Unless you are a Buddha or a monk with the opportunity to chant all day, the whole "quieting your thoughts" thing is pretty much a myth. I mean, have you actually tried that? It just makes things worse. (This is different from noticing your thoughts and letting them pass on by, which is taught in many mediation practices.)

Many of us drank or used drugs or whatever the addiction of the moment in order to try and escape our thinking. Guess what happens when we stop doing the thing that was keeping the thoughts at bay? Yeah, I know. It's like an avalanche of thoughts all tumbling around over and over, and you are smothered by them with no hope of escape.

Meadow DeVor says, "Don't do the thing you usually do and see what comes up."

Time does heal some wounds, and the length of sobriety can definitely make a difference in taming the mind monster. But as you probably know—since you are reading this book—it doesn't completely do the job.

Michael Singer, author of *The Untethered Soul*, calls all this thinking, your "inner roommate." He relates an exercise of just observing the conversations you have with yourself and bearing witness. If you were to actually speak this internal conversation out loud, you would appear to be a loon. Try it for a moment. It's quite enlightening.

Observer, Witness, Spirit, or Soul

What if I told you that you are not your thoughts? You are neither your body nor your emotions either. There is another portion of you that, if you think about it (pun intended), is separate from all of these parts that make up this person you know as you.

Some religions call this your Spirit or Soul. Others call it the Observer or Witness. And some say we have both.

Ram Dass says that the Witness is actually another level of consciousness—that this part of you is awareness of your own thoughts, feelings, and emotions.

Becoming Aware of your Thoughts

What do you do about this avalanche of thoughts, which is making you crazier than ever and seems to be making all of your problems worse as well?

One of the easiest tools found in many meditation and yoga practices is noticing the thoughts as they float into your mind and then letting them float on out. Just notice your thoughts, like you do smells or sounds. When you become aware that you just followed a thought out into the universe or to the mall, bring your awareness back to your breath or the sensation of your feet on the ground.

I like to imagine clouds floating by, setting the thoughts on a cloud, and letting them float away.

You may have noticed that you become much more relaxed, calmer, and not as bombarded by your thoughts when you do the Grounding and Boundaries exercise. If not, that's OK. Just keep at it.

You can start with baby steps on all of these processes. Just start somewhere. This is not a race. There is no time crunch. And there are many, many rewards for establishing some sort of practice.

My client Jo, a devout student of much that is spiritual, and I had a laugh when discovering that neither of us practices all of these methods all of the time. But we do *something* all of the time. When we stop picking on ourselves for spiritual imperfection and stop making it some new sort of competition, we can relax into our own luminous nature.

Breath Control (Pranayama) and Yoga

Those Yogis, they know a thing or two. The word *yoga* means "to yoke" or "connect." Yoga connects the body and the mind through the breath. I will stress over and over how important yoga is to healing your entire being from the stress and problems of trauma and addiction. It is absolutely one of the top magical potions for calming your body and your mind.

And, if you are like me and most of my clients, you can't practice yoga twenty-four-seven. Nor do you want to.

You can breathe though, and breath control is just as powerful as yoga in calming the mind. This breath control is called *pranayama* and it's pretty fantastic!

One of the easiest, most effective methods of breath control is Belly Breathing. You can do it anywhere and at any time—and you may just find yourself with a new career as a musician, since this is how singers breathe. If you watch babies sleeping, you will notice how the belly rises and falls, not the chest.

Just for fun, take a deep breath. Hold it. Where did the air go? Did your belly expand or your chest? If it was your chest, don't feel bad—you are like most people who have been told to take a deep breath. We breathe into our chest—which, since it's a deep breath, is somewhat better than short, shallow breathing—but it's not optimal. Chest breathing is stress-response breathing and can activate your fight or flight response. This is why taking deep breaths into your chest doesn't come with the desired calming effect.

Now, try placing both hands on your belly. Take a slow, measured deep breath *into* the belly. Make sure the belly expands. Then on the exhale, push the air out by contracting the belly. Breathe this way a couple more times and then begin to add a four count rhythm. Inhale to the count of four, hold for four, exhale to the count of four, hold for four, and repeat. Make sure the belly expands on the inhale and contracts on the exhale. This may take you awhile to get the hang of, as most people automatically breathe the opposite way in our stress-responsive, hold-in-your-belly-to-look-skinny culture.

Keep at this. You will notice that it really works. This breathing style is excellent for helping with anxiety at any time of day or with insomnia at any time of night.

There are many other pranayama techniques, such as alternate nostril breathing and ujjayi breathing. I've chosen not to go over them here to keep these Magic Keys simple and easy to use, but you can look up pranayama practices on-line or in any book on the subject.

Thought Work

Thought Work, a process in which you deeply question your thoughts, was founded by Byron Katie in 1986. It is a phenomenal method of self-inquiry and questioning. Through doing The Work process, you can transform your thinking and your beliefs. The Work process can be found for free on-line. I use this process religiously on my own thoughts and beliefs, and my coach helps me question my own beliefs as well. I highly recommend you try it, although, it seems to be much easier to understand and work through the process with a guide, such as your own coach. Funny how other people can see through your thinking and beliefs better than you can yourself.

As Melecia grows into the best version of herself, she has naturally begun to feel more emotions, to notice when certain situations don't feel quite right for her, and to question her thoughts. On one occasion, she came in feeling uncomfortable about a situation that had occurred at the school where she teaches. There had been a decision to move her back into a former classroom, and Melecia felt good about this decision. What felt weird was she was not informed about the change directly. She learned of it through other teachers and then at a school meeting. I determined that we could successfully use Thought Work in this situation. The conversation that follows is a walk-through of the Thought Work process.

MEL: "She should've told me."

ME: "Is it true that she should've told you?"

MEL: "Yes."

ME: "Can you absolutely know that it's true that she should've told you?"

MEL: "Yes."

ME: "When you believe/think the thought "she should've told me" does it bring you stress or peace?"

MEL: "Stress."

ME: "How do you feel when you think and believe the thought? Do you feel emotions? Where? What are they? Do any images come up? Do any obsessions or addictions appear? How do you treat the person? How do you treat yourself?"

MEL: "Wow. I feel irritated and annoyed. This feels heavy in my chest and the color is red. I over eat, mostly sweets, and I avoid her. I pick on myself by overeating and by not acknowledging my feelings or being an adult and just going and talking to her."

ME: "Who you would be without the thought, "she should've told me"?"

MEL: "I would just be me, enjoying the job that I love.

I wouldn't be overeating and avoiding."

ME: "Now turn around the original thought in three ways and give three supporting statements for each new thought."

MEL: "1. She should've told me and its OK that I think that. a) It directly affects me. b) She makes the decisions. c) Others knew. 2. She shouldn't have told me. a) It's her decision to make. b) She's human and maybe felt uncomfortable too. c) She may not have been 100 percent on board with her decision and was doing it to give me what I want. 3. I should've told me. a) I could've asked when I heard from others. b) I can acknowledge myself and do grown-up things. c) I don't have to hide from myself or others."

I then asked Melecia which of these turn-arounds was more accurate for her. She was able to realize that she played a part in the uncomfortable situation at her work and that she was able to be seen, acknowledge herself, and do the grown-up things.

If you are experiencing trouble with your thoughts and blaming yourself and others for problems in your life, Thought Work is a very good resource to help you uncover a deeper truth. This practice brings much solace to our overworked minds.

Nature and Space

I feel nature saved me. I grew up herding cows and riding rodeo, and even though I moved to the big city and became a party girl, I always found solace in nature. Snowboarding, jet skiing, running, playing with pets, and generally loving being outdoors kept me from completely losing all touch with my inner guide. As a matter of fact, the times I was too messed up or too hungover to be outside made me feel worse than ever.

As a sober person, I spend more time outdoors than ever before with a gentle focus on noticing the simple mysteries. How does that leaf get so green? What did my dog just smell? My eyes can see to the curvature of the valley and beyond. The pink and orange and yellow of the sunset feel like home. Getting outside calms my mind and it will yours as well. No phones or music allowed—just you and your earth home.

Putting It All Together

Give yourself some space to breathe and sit and just be. Problems sort themselves out when we back off, stop trying to control everything, and slow down a little—and then slow down a little more than that.

Learn some easy yoga poses, get outside, take space, do your Grounding and Boundaries practice out in nature, and notice how your mind begins to calm down. I love to do Thought Work on my problematic thinking while I am running trails. Whether you are a beginner or a seasoned veteran of these types of practices, I find great insight in writing out my thoughts. You can catch some pretty obvious "stinking thinking" on paper. Then, instead of pushing these thoughts aside or making yourself wrong, you can make sense of them with the power of Thought Work.

Bring to mind an actual warrior you admire, maybe a martial artist. Notice how focused and strong they are as they train and then go into battle. They train their minds, as well as their bodies. This is Magic Key #1. Become a Thought Warrior.

Chapter Five—Magic Key #2: Your Body *Is* the Key

Lilly made her way into my practice after eighteen long and painful months of going from doctor to doctor and receiving no real answers for why she was in such excruciating pain. She could barely walk from the agony in her left groin and hip, which was supposedly nerve damage from a severe bout of shingles. Coming to see me was a last resort or she was considering surgery that she wasn't sure was going to help.

Lilly is another who experienced boundary impairment as a young girl. She never had a place to feel safe, other than excelling in business and school. Here, she could escape and get an "A" and feel she was doing OK.

Only, she wasn't doing OK at all. She was completely disconnected from her body and emotions. She was running on adrenaline, pain medications, and fear. She felt out of options and "did not want to live this life anymore." Our first session was spent with Grounding and Boundaries work, creating a safe space for her and her traumatized body and mind.

Lilly's methods of distraction and disassociation— disordered eating, cycling drug and alcohol abuse, and excessive working—had come to a screeching halt. Her body said "enough" and very creatively used extreme pain to make her pay attention.

With the level of pain that Lilly was experiencing, the most supportive of restorative yoga poses were necessary. Messages in the form of images began to appear for her to decipher. The pain in her hip and groin gave a picture of a "tug of war" between her husband and daughter, as well as between her husband and their two dogs, with her in the middle. This picture was very revealing of the type of relationship Lilly had experienced with all of the men in her life. She was constantly feeling "in trouble" and under enormous amounts of pressure to perform. As a young girl, she lived in constant fear of making her dad angry and was experiencing the same fear in her marriage.

At this time, I didn't know if Lilly would continue to use her new tools on a regular basis. She said, "I want to change—I'm so unhappy." Yet, in each session she also spoke of being terrified to leave her unhappy marriage, as she's "afraid I'm going to die." She had one foot in and one foot out, another "tug of war."

Your body carries the entire universe inside. You are made of the clay and dirt of the earth. In the noise of the world and what we are "supposed" to be, do, say, look and act—we get lost. We don't know how to listen to the Voice of the Body.

The Body Voice speaks slowly. It speaks in images, sensations, memories, and colors. Since the body is the part of you always in the present moment, it contains your entire history and tells the truth. The body is your story, and it is one of the most profound messengers available to you. In our culture, we have a tendency to bully, poke, prod, starve, cut, punish, ignore, poison, and look at our "earth home" in disgust. Funny, that's sort of how we treat our planet too, isn't it?

If I could give you a gift straight out of the pages of this book, I would give you the ability and desire to befriend your body.

I feel such deep sadness as I write this. There is grief for how I treated my own body for so long—grief for the times I still forget that it only wants to take care of me. Tears flow for the gratitude I feel for a body that, at middle age, still takes such good care of me. Even in sobriety, before I become more grounded and aware, I starved my beautiful home. I hated it daily.

I don't know the answer to when we became so disconnected. If I think too much on the enormity of the problem, I get overwhelmed and convinced I can't really do anything to help.

But, I'm putting on my warrior pants and knowing the truth. If I heal a little more every day and I watch others around me healing, then I have to keep going. It is my duty to give this knowledge to all that can hear it.

Again, part of the answer is patience, space, and time to let the body talk. I used to do this thing where I would ask my body, "What do you want to tell me?" And then I wouldn't wait for the answer.

The knowledge that the body doesn't so much speak in words as in images is part of deciphering the body's voice. Holding long, slow, gentle restorative yoga poses and knowing what questions to ask gives the body time and space to answer. Knowing how to unlock the message in an image the body gives you is obviously very important. You can ask, "What does this image mean to me?" and receive valuable information. Processes such as Myth Metaphor work can help you go deeper into what your body is trying to tell you.

The location of the pain, injury or illness also gives huge clues. For example, if you are experiencing lower back pain—you know the root and sacral chakras are related to that area and that those chakras are associated with finances, home, survival, creativity, and the right to have and feel pleasure—and you realize you are broke, working all of the time, and not having any fun—you would know that the body is asking you to pay attention to what is going on in those areas of your life.

Many people go through life not even wondering if their heart attack was caused by a "broken heart" or if the throat cancer Grandma had came from never using her voice or expressing how she really felt.

The famous author Louise Hay wrote one of the most respected and well-loved accounts of the mind-body connection in *You Can Heal Your Life*. I personally don't know of a body-based healer that doesn't reference this beautiful book.

Another brilliant line of body questioning comes from Dr. John E. Sarno in *Healing Back Pain: The Mind-Body Connection*. He believes that pain and illness come from the mistaken belief that our bodies are not strong (after millions of years of living evidence to the contrary) and from fear of more pain. He suggests we have a conversation with our body. We can tell it that we are listening and that we know it is trying to distract us from our fear and anxiety. We can thank our bodies for protecting us and let our bodies know that "I'm a big person, I'm listening and I don't need you to distract me anymore, because I can handle this situation." I have used this process to great success over the last year, since I read the book. It's pretty fascinating!

How do you learn to listen to your own body as a Magic Key? Well, the books and thoughts I've mentioned above are all super helpful. Here are some other ways you can begin to befriend your body and listen to its messages.

Note: When you receive a message from your body and you don't listen or follow through on the message, you are in effect telling your body, "I heard you, and I don't care." Clearly, this is not such a great idea if you want your body to continue communicating with you in a friendly manner.

Your Body Is an Animal

Truly, your body is an animal. It wants love, protection, good food and water, shelter, and movement. It wants to be comforted when it is sad or scared. It wants attention when it is sick or injured. It wants rest when it is tired. It wants physical touch and sensations that feel good. How would you comfort a cold, scared, lost puppy or child? That is how you can learn to give your body gentle, reassuring, self-care. This will restore your love and affection for your "animal."

This Magic Key may feel tough to implement initially. Take your time. Try a new practice daily. Ask your body what it wants to do for movement (instead of forcing it). The indigenous peoples and our ancestors did not separate their bodies from the earth or nature. They knew the body was just as much a part of the landscape as rocks or trees.

It's a beautiful journey, this adventure of loving the body, and it's well worth the treasure chest of rewards you will receive.

Yoga

Yoga was very instrumental in helping me heal the hatred and disgust for my body. Yoga is stealthy. It slyly works its magic on the practitioner, bringing in more self-love, self-awareness, and presence. I still don't fully understand how it does that, but it does. Trust me. Just go. Restorative yoga was where I learned that in order to *really* listen and hear what my body had to say, I needed more time and space than I had ever given it before. I needed someone to help me ask the right questions and *wait* for the answers.

Chakra-Related Questions for the Body

A core concept for learning to receive information from your body is through using questions that are associated with each chakra. Combining restorative yoga poses and these questions (suggested restorative yoga poses corresponding with each chakra and the related question can be found by visiting my website and emailing me a request—I'll send you a free video of the process) along with space and time is a profound manner of receiving guidance from your body.

The following examples are taken from individual client sessions.

Root Chakra: If you have addiction problems (even if you are sober), you have root chakra issues. This chakra is related to finances, safety, home, and stability. Root chakra hardships can also present as problems in the lower pelvis, legs, knees, and feet.

Lilly is a good example of hidden root chakra problems. At first glance she is very stable, because she's always been able to "have" money. But, she has never felt safe and that eventually presented as the pain in the groin, hip, and legs.

Rian had a history of financial difficulty and instability, although she was almost always employable. She still grapples with figuring out a steady stream of income that reflects her education and skill set.

Since the basic right of this chakra is "to be here and to have," and since fear is always a component of instability, the questions to ask here are, "What are you afraid of?" and "What action needs to be taken?"

Lilly begins to expand and take charge of her life

when she focuses on strengthening her Grounding and Boundaries as a regular "action," being faced with the daily fear that her relationship brings. She can begin to protect herself and not run away into work. Her pain decreases. She has weaned herself off of pain medication during our work together.

Rian must budget and perform "adult actions," like paying attention to clearing up past money problems, in order to face her root chakra fear. She checks in often with how she is feeling. She knows from our coaching that overwhelm is a choice, so she works through these feelings instead of becoming more disconnected from what she must take care of. She makes sure to play as well, as fun balances out the heaviness of being a grown-up.

Sacral Chakra: Guilt and shame are the issues in the sacral chakra difficulty, and they follow us all the way into and through sobriety. This makes sense as the basic right is "to feel and have pleasure." Most, if not all, of our addiction processes come from the desire to feel "better" no matter what the cost. We start out with guilt and shame, try to numb those feelings, and end up with enough guilt and shame to drown in it.

At three years sober, in a session with my own coach, I was feeling an enormous amount of shame over things I had done in the past. I had made amends and was still walking around trying to make up for being a "shitty person." I was exhausted, resentful, and wanted to hide.

Zena was trying to place all the people in her family

in strategic positions, so that they wouldn't fight and argue. She spent an enormous amount of energy trying to make sure certain people weren't in the same room with each other. At first glance this would appear to be a control issue, yet there's more.

"Who has been hurt?" and "What must be made right?" are the questions to ask for issues in the sacral chakra. The compassion inherent in these questions can bring about the sweet release of sadness as it did for both me and Zena.

I was able to see that I really had done enough. I have reconnected with my family. I pay where payment is due and help others however I can. I don't have to hurt myself or anyone else further by not having boundaries, overdoing, and trying so hard to be liked that I do things not in alignment with my own standards. I can and do have the power to make things right.

Zena had an aha moment when we asked these questions in relation to "controlling" her family dynamics. She had been shamed as a young person, and making sure everyone got along was a way for her to feel OK. She had been put in positions of parenting herself and manipulating to get the slightest amount of attention. Of course she was going to continue to play out these patterns as an adult in order to feel "enough." She was able to see that she was the one who had been hurt and that she could make things right by taking care of her own needs and leaving her family to sort out their own stuff.

Solar Plexus Chakra: This area is your will to get things done, self-esteem, and confidence. The basic right is "to act and be an individual." The problem here is also with shame. Physically, the presentation can be with digestive disorders, chronic fatigue, pancreatitis, liver, and gall bladder problems. The person with low self-esteem and co-dependency aggravations most likely has as a solar plexus chakra hardship. It is also common for them to have eating disorders, either currently or in the past.

Lisa (who you will meet in chapter six) really wants to make things OK for everybody. She was never taught that she had any importance, instead informed that the way to get along in the world was to give up her own needs entirely. She would bail out her twin daughters financially and emotionally to the great detriment of her own health and financial security.

Lilly, with a past and present mired in shame, presented with a history of anorexia and, of course, with the ever-present need to "get the A" in order to prove her self-worth. It was the only way she could feel good about herself.

When one has a healthy and balanced solar plexus chakra, they are confident, warm, and with appropriate self-discipline. They are good at setting personal boundaries. You probably wouldn't describe them as a door-mat. Neither Lisa nor Lilly had these qualities on a regular basis. They could fake it for a while, especially back when they were in active addiction. Sobriety can bring those faux walls crumbling down. We are left staring at patterns, enmeshment, and emotions that we don't know what to do with.

This is why the solar plexus chakra questions, "What needs to be protected?" and, "What must be restored?" are usually mind-bendy and transformative.

Lisa realized she needed to protect herself, her new marriage, and her money from her daughters. She also needed to stop fixing everything for them, so they could grow up. She related that her mother had treated her in this manner. Lisa had not learned to stand on her own two feet. She in turn passed this behavior to her daughters, both of whom ended up repeating the family history of addiction (they are all clean and sober now). By restoring her own personal boundaries, Lisa is teaching her children new patterns. She is breaking the cycle, which is gratifying for all, as she has a new grandbaby.

Lilly had to start protecting herself from her ingrained pattern of self-abuse and self-shame. She was so drained of life-force, she believed every negative thing that her family said about her. This had been a vicious cycle for many years, and her body had called a halt to it all. It took us many sessions of partnership with the body so that she could set up protections for herself. She loves the boundary exercise and gets in her "bubble" often. She was able to restore herself by taking a two week vacation alone with her two dogs. This from the woman who thought she was going to "die" if she was alone.

Heart Chakra: The dear human heart. It is capable

of the greatest acts of love, empathy and compassion, while also holding lifetimes of grief. Physical problems with the heart chakra include heart attacks, breast and chest problems, and tension between the shoulder blades. The person with heart chakra problems can be cold and numb or caught in debilitating loss and grief. The basic right is "to love and be loved."

Shelby, my colleague, was adopted at birth by a great family who showed unconditional love. She first noticed she was unable to feel happy at thirty-five years of age. She felt numb and flat-lined. She just wasn't enjoying any of the things she usually liked doing.

While Rian certainly hasn't had the hardest life of any human on the planet, she had been subject to much loss. Drugs, alcohol, and disordered eating had kept the grief at a distance. She had gained weight in sobriety and was cycling again into fad dieting and extreme exercise in an attempt to regain some sort of control. The fixation on her weight had worked before to push away uncomfortable feelings, including loss and self-loathing.

The life of an addict almost inherently contains loss or never having been loved at all. It is one of the main reasons we want to numb and ease the pain. If we make it out of our personal hell, the heart chakra questions, "What needs to be loved?" and, "What wants to be released?" can provide much sought after comfort and understanding.

Through our yoga and coaching training Shelby was able to cry for the first time in years. Shelby has continued on with therapy and coaching. Her body showed an image of a protective wall around her heart. She realized she had this "wall" all of her life, which would be appropriate as she was born into the "saddest place you can be." This wall is also a fortress around the other emotions. Her on-going work with the wall includes staying in the present moment when she notices it, or when she's not able to feel anything. Since the wall has been an appropriate survival skill, the thing she doesn't want to do is to try to change the presence of the wall or to make it go away. She has to sit with and feel the wall and the emotions it is protecting her from. This wall is her friend. It needs to be loved, just as her other emotions do.

When asked "What needs to be loved?" Rian's body showed us an image of her as an already anorexic teen. Through communication with her body, Rian has been able to remember that her body is just asking for love. It is not an easy process for Rian, to release the confines of body perfectionism and just love her "animal" self. She is making great strides and hasn't food restricted in over a year. She is patient and kind with her body, which happens to be responding with weight stabilization and balance.

The other three chakras have corresponding questions, which are utilized as needed. In the early stages of uncovering why sober life can be so hard, we tend to work almost exclusively in the lower four chakras, the ones just covered. This is, in part, because we are growing ourselves up—we are giving ourselves the parenting we didn't receive. We follow the guidelines of the chakra system to do this. Another reason is so that you can remain in your body more and more often. Your body responds gratefully, feeling and functioning more optimally. Staying grounded and in relation to your body keeps you from overthinking and causing yourself more hardship. Remember, your body is the one you can trust. It always tells the truth.

I've made the choice to not cover the questions for the upper chakras here, because we tend to "live" there anyway in our lives of disconnection. I want you to focus almost exclusively on chakras one through four.

I'm so excited for you now, having established such good Grounding and Boundaries practices. This is good Sober Warrior training. And you get to move on to our next Magic Key . . .

Shall we proceed?

Chapter Six—Magic Key #3:
Emotional Messengers

I hadn't seen Lisa in years, although I knew we had both taken the sober path. She had been a chiropractic patient of mine, years ago. I was thrilled to receive her message stating she wanted to work on some issues she was having in her recovery.

She says, "I was coming up on my four year chip for sobriety from alcohol. And even though I had completed my twelve steps twice through my Celebrate Recovery classes at my church, I was still struggling with anger and codependency. I was sober, though sometimes I was just angry, because I felt like things should be easier and better—and they were, but I also felt that somehow I should be farther along in my recovery. Now I had to really feel things and deal with them and couldn't just numb it out anymore. I was even co-leading classes and sponsoring girls. How could anyone learn from me? I was still messed up and still searching for something."

Lisa was grappling with understanding her emotions. She was angry and then felt guilty and ashamed for those feelings. She just didn't know where to turn. She was feeling bad, because so much of the time we are told to "just be good or nice or happy," and she wasn't feeling any of those things much of the time. It didn't seem real or possible.

The Heart Voice

Your heart has a voice, and its voice is your emotions. Your heart is the valve that lets you feel. Your feelings are your emotions. When your heart is closed, you are numb and disconnected. When your heart is open, you are feeling your feelings—even the so called "negative" or "bad" emotions. You are still feeling!

Emotions have become much maligned. They are thought of as "too much" in our culture. We are told not to be "too" emotional, nor to bottle up our emotions. This is confusing at best.

Pre-sobriety, I did all I could to avoid feeling anything. The only time I could cry was during a sad movie or book, when the animal was killed or injured. I was numb and disassociated most of the time. Drugs made me really not feel, so it was very easy to cut myself off from people or situations that hurt. My addictions made it simple to push down and push away all feelings. If they threatened to well-up inside me, I would find some way to act out an addiction, so I couldn't feel the panic that would arise.

When I went through periods of anger, fear, and depression when I wasn't using, I had a great excuse for why I was feeling that way—addiction abuse and the resulting low. I honestly thought I was only feeling these things because of the chemical unbalance in my body and brain from the weekend party.

When I finally got sober, I could only name and feel anger, fear, sadness, and happiness. The wide range of emotional vocabulary was not available to me. I had lost that skill. I was also still operating under the false and dangerous belief that the goal was to be happy—all of the time.

Happy All the Time

The new age, positive thinking, law of attraction mindset—while valid and powerful—can set us up for a dangerous belief system. It doesn't validate or leave much room for our necessary and compelling emotional guidance.

We aren't taught to question our operating systems. Positive thinking can be quite enticing for a person who loves to distract their self from what is really going on. For someone with a history of trauma or addiction (most of us), just thinking, "Everything is going to be alright," isn't true or helpful.

Pushing aside our emotions invalidates and represses them, making our efforts to "be happy" and "think positive" a lie. Everything can look pretty on the outside, but we destroy our connection to our truth and our boundaries, and we create more pressure and stress.

Something has to give, and it does. One experiences an explosion of rage or grief as an outward expression of emotions. Or, the emotions are turned inward causing internal boundary destruction and damage.

Either way, we are overwhelmed by stress and more pressure to buck up, get control, and act properly. Addictions and obsessions appear to help us calm down, but then nothing gets resolved and the cycle begins again.

What we need is a process of honoring our Heart Voice. We must acknowledge, express, and give voice to our feelings. We need to create safety in order to do this. We need to be vulnerable with ourselves first and then with others.

This process takes us back to Grounding and Boundaries and chakra work. We can use emotional inquiry to gain the knowledge that Magic Key #3 has for us.

Emotions are neither good nor bad. They are just emotions. They are part of what makes us human. To turn away from them is to turn away from our humanity.

Karla McLaren, in *The Language of Emotions,* gives us the questions for each emotion. It's hard for me to understand how I ever managed to get through any emotional situation without the gift of knowledge that this book offers. I actually didn't manage my emotions well at all, as I expressed earlier. This book, and the processes I use for myself and in my coaching, has changed my relationship with myself and others in a profound way.

Messages in Your Emotions

You will want to be grounded and set up with strong boundaries when you begin this work. Notice that I am asking you to keep grounding. Keep using those Boundary practices. You want them to become second nature when you are calm and quiet, so you can remember and access your tools when you are in a highly stressful situation. I recommend you also read or listen to McLaren's book to strengthen your knowledge and emotional practice. You are going to need it to help yourself on this journey of sorting your sober life problems.

Grab your adventurer hat and let's go!

Anger: *What must be protected? What must be restored?*

Anger is an active, fiery emotion that arises when your boundaries have been crossed. It alerts you and tells you that you need to pay attention to something going on around you or in you. If your anger is directed outward, your attention needs to go toward strengthening your boundaries and sorting out whom or what is crossing them. If your anger is directed inward, you have crossed your own boundaries and will want to slow down and pay attention. Anger can help you heal your trauma and help you set proper boundaries. Rage and fury are also part of this realm. Working with your anger can assist you in understanding anger in others. I used to be terrified of anger in others, because I was always repressing my own. "*I'm* not an angry person." Now, I can sit with my own anger and the anger of others and honor it. I don't try to "make nice" and repress my anger or the anger of others.

Lisa is a kind and gentle soul, and this anger thing was really tearing her up. She said to me, "Why can't I just pull it together?"

I told her, "Anger is an indication that boundaries are being crossed."

Lisa was astounded. She realized she had no structure around herself. She was trying to do everything for everybody, exhausting herself being a door-mat. Then she would explode. She was caught in a cycle of repression and expression and confused about why she was acting so crazy.

Step one was to teach her to protect herself (boundaries) and restore her sense of self (grounding). She has also been pleased with being able to integrate the knowledge that her feelings and emotions are very "human" and are quite normal.

Guilt and Shame: *Who has been hurt? What must be made right?*

Guilt and shame are two of the emotions that addicts of any kind experience. We take pills or watch porn or eat gallons of ice cream to avoid feeling something. Then shame arises to help us realize we are hurting ourselves. We don't want to feel that shame (ugh!), so we numb out again to push it away. It's a vicious and much misunderstood cycle.

We get into discovery and start the beautiful, painful process of healing and putting our lives back together. The process of right action and asking for forgiveness from those we have hurt puts some of the puzzle pieces back in place. For many people, it is not the whole story or process. Society and families shame us. Maybe your body or appearance is one of your greatest sources of shame. Maybe you have stopped drinking and now can't stop overeating or gambling or smoking cigarettes, and you just feel icky. Why, if I've stopped my biggest "hook," can't I stop this one?

Guilt tends to put us on alert when we are about to do something wrong according to our moral code. Instead of trying to push it away, if you can stop and question, "Should I do something different?" then you will be guided to the next right action. It's a sort of stop sign. You can also ask if this guilt is someone else's moral code. For example, if you feel guilty when you don't finish all the food on your plate, yet you are full and you don't want more food, whose idea is that?

Shame follows on the heels of guilt if we proceed. If we are aware, grounded and clear in our sobriety, shame should feel like an internal fire. You will probably wish the ground could swallow you up, will get all hot and flustered, and will want to disappear. Sadly, we don't really know what to do with this emotion, as most of us were taught about shame by being shamed. Shame impairs our boundaries. Addiction shaming and body shaming, so prominent in this digital culture, are two of the largest and most detrimental shaming practices evident today.

Guilt and shame can and should follow an outburst of anger as we described in Lisa's case above. But, if we never learn the information held in the emotions, it becomes a perpetual cycle—explode, feel ashamed, apologize, feel confused, repress and erupt again.

Lisa realized she had been hurt by conditioning in childhood where she learned that repression ("being nice") was her only option in sticky situations. She has begun taking responsibility for her emotions and is making things "right" by addressing her own behavior.

Fear: *What action should be taken?*

Fear includes anxiety and worry. Fear protects us from danger. Your fear is present all of the time, you just don't know it. Fear helps you move out of the way of scary people and situations, jump to the side if something is thrown at you, and run or freeze when you need to. Your body takes over and gets you moving or hiding before you may even realize it. It's a primal response and we need it.

When you are grounded and aware, you can feel fear and ask yourself what you need to do in the situation. Even doing nothing is an action.

Sadly, we have been taught to "feel the fear and do it anyway" and ignore your feelings because they are "too emotional." So we tell fear to go away and then we get in big trouble. You can still do something that brings up fear, but you'll want to pause and ask the question, "What action needs to be taken?" and make sure that you take aware action. Fear is a brilliant and powerful messenger that will help you solve many of your problems.

When I notice that I am procrastinating or distracting from something I don't want to do, I can now realize that fear is probably underneath my inaction. I can then deftly ask, "What am I afraid of?" It typically has to do with the story of "not being good enough." Now I can inquire, "What action needs to be taken?" Maybe it's a tough phone call or putting myself out there in the world in a bigger way. Gently and compassionately, I can walk beside the part of me that is afraid. I can help this part do what needs to be done without being mean to her. Maybe it's one phone call, instead of five. This alleviates the fear and pressure, yet helps me to acknowledge what my emotions are telling me.

Panic and terror are also fear based emotions and are anchored in the healing of trauma. They are powerful and can come from unresolved traumas that have been frozen in the body. Working with a trained practitioner is very effective in moving these strong emotions.

Sadness: *What must be released? What must be rejuvenated?*

Permission to feel my sadness and *not* make myself wrong for it, or let others make me wrong, has been one the most empowered gifts of my sober journey. Adulthood and addiction robbed me of my ability to truly release and feel sad and then be restored.

Sadness lets you cry, heal, and mend. Sadness gives you back your love and compassion for yourself and others. Sadness brings with it the healing power of rejuvenation, which then gives you back your strength.

Lilly cried throughout most of our initial sessions. She had been pushing down emotions for too many years. Giving her permission to release her sadness was a giant step toward healing her pain. Sometimes, we really must just cry. It's more than OK—it is appropriate. Rejuvenation follows release and can be performed mindfully by imagining yourself in a special safe place (inside your boundary) being filled with earth energy.

Grief: *What must be mourned? What must be released completely?*

When grief goes unexpressed after deep loss, it gets buried and ignored, which can damage the psyche. Babies die, relationships end, and our beloved pets are tragically killed. If we don't allow ourselves to feel the grief and dive into the river of all souls' pain, we miss out on the healing that is necessary. We disconnect and lose ourselves in soul-numbingly ordinary, addicted, distracted lives.

If your problems in sobriety (or active addiction) stem in part from unexpressed grief, you will not carry out your life's purpose or destiny. You must be courageous and mourn and release your loss completely. You will not die or get stuck there as you fear. Instead, you are stuck in not letting go. The pain of numbness is greater than the pain of feeling your grief. You just don't know it yet.

Honorable grieving is not taught to many of us. Zena was still grieving her interrupted childhood and the death of her sister. She didn't even know this, since the pain was buried under layers of addiction. As she grows into a grounded individual, she is able to heal and comfort those aspects of herself that were so neglected. She can let grief transform as it needs to without disrupting the process of her life.

The process of grieving can be assisted by a trained professional and is suggested.

Depression: *Where has my energy gone? Why was it sent away?*

Severe depression is no joke and should not be ignored. Please seek professional help if you have long term depression. A combination of medication, body-work, therapy, coaching, movement, essential oils, and being in nature may be in order. Depression is a sign to stop and pay attention to something. This something is most likely a gathering of emotions and situations you did not want to notice.

Situational depression is also a stop sign. Our culture has become far too dependent on drugs to "fix" our emotions. When sad things happen, we should stop for a moment and acknowledge that an event has occurred. When you lose an important job or opportunity and you are feeling appropriately sad, it would be weird if you didn't feel that way.

Writing this book was a big stretch for me, in so many areas. I've had to become an author and a grown-up. I didn't plan to write this book. It just sort of happened. I broke my financial sobriety (chapter eight) to write it. I thought writing and having a book would solve all my problems, which is magical thinking at its best. I lost my connection with my grounding, and I began to distract and disconnect from all of my emotions. I was writing and running and drinking too much coffee and watching Netflix just to not feel the embarrassment, shame, fear, and elation underneath all the activity. I had no idea how to be adult enough to work this hard, and I was terrified I had messed up more royally while sober than ever before.

My body's wisdom stepped up to the plate. I got very

sick with a severe head cold. Then depression showed up. My experience with depression has mostly been related to reasons I could understand. But I didn't understand this, because I was so busy hiding from all my other emotions. My very talented Coach/ Somatic Psychotherapist, Jodi Krahn, stepped in to help. We worked a session and uncovered the thoughts and emotions that I was ignoring. Jodi reminded me about the message always found in depression. I learned that my energy had been "sent to the mountains" while I sorted things out, so that I wouldn't continue to distract and destroy all I had built in my years of sobriety.

Our emotional messengers bring stunning insight and gifts to the party when we are open to receiving them. Depression is no exception.

Happiness

And you thought we were just going to talk about the "not so fun" stuff. Happiness is a celebration and a thank-you. It *is* fun and should absolutely be felt and enjoyed. Being sober is a celebration in itself, because the load is so much lighter. So feel happy and play, celebrate and laugh! Just don't get caught in the trap of thinking that you *should and must stay here at all costs.* That is a slippery slope and a lie. If we are happy all of the time, then how do we know we are happy, because we don't have anything to compare it to? Just enjoy happy—don't try to *make* happy happen. It is just like all of the other emotions: it's not here to stay, but it will be back.

What a relief it has been to not have to be happy all of the time. Now when happiness arrives, it is so much more fun, because I am not trying desperately to get it to stick around. It is also a neat gauge for other emotions and helps me pay attention to what is going on around and within me.

Contentment

Contentment is that lovely feeling of warmth and appreciation that arrives after a job or a challenge well-done. Contentment will unpack its suitcase after you have worked really hard on something, allowing you to sit back, enjoy the fruits of your labor, and prepare for your next mission. Contentment rewards you and reminds you that you have faithfully traveled on the right path. Sing the songs of gratitude into the night and rest dear traveler—you have come a long way.

I feel content quite often these days, like after a yoga session or magical run. I feel it when the words flow onto the page or when I finish reading a book that changes my life.

Acknowledging and playing with your Heart Voice is a magical, rewarding part of your adventurer's backpack. It can be a superpower, enabling you to come "home" wherever you are. You may still have emotional problems and melt-downs, but they will not come as surprises or take you into the chaos of overwhelm.

Listen! Can you hear the last Magic Key calling your name?

Chapter Seven— Magic Key #4: The Voice of Your Soul

The voice of your soul has been called higher power, God, spirit, soul, divine, nature, destiny, intuition, and much more. It speaks in a whisper. Getting to where we can clearly hear this voice is why we cultivate such practices as prayer, yoga, being in nature, movement, dancing, and laughing. Your Soul Voice is the voice that got you sober. It is the voice that encouraged you to buy this book. It gives you guidance when you don't even know you need it.

Spirituality and spiritual programs are not linear, although we are very encouraged to think so. Instead, your natural rhythms and inclinations for spiritual practice are more circular. Native American and Celtic wisdom (to name a just a couple) believed that our entire being was connected to all of the landscape and stars and so benefited from a circular path. This journey contained peaks and valleys, yet there was always progress because you couldn't go backward. It is a gentler look at your progress and challenges.

In *Anam Cara: A Book of Celtic Wisdom*, John O'Donohue states, "The spiritual life is imagined as a journey with a sequence of stages. Each stage has its own methodology, negativity and possibilities. Such a program often becomes an end in itself. It weighs our natural presence against us. Such a program can divide and separate us from what is most commonly ours. The past is forsaken as irredeemable—the present is used as the fulcrum to a future that bodes holiness, integration, or perfection. When time is reduced to linear progress, it is emptied of presence."

In simpler terms, your path is *your* path. It is unique, divinely guided, and neither straight nor narrow. You can release the pressure of moving forward and backward on some imaginary straight line of spiritual and personal perfection. And, your past does not need to be "forsaken as irredeemable."

Your unique destiny and problems are intertwined. I know of very few humans who are willing to take a clear look at what their problems are trying to tell them whom doesn't learn beautiful messages and purposes from those problems. Their issues become how they live—to help others and make a difference.

The Soul Voice wants you to let it come to you, instead of you trying to force it by a rigorous linear spiritual practice. By surrendering to each threshold you are brought to, this Magic Key can transform your life and your response to living.

I find the simple, quiet, spacious beauty of nature lets my Soul Voice join me on my path. Even if you live in the darkest of places devoid of natural beauty, you can plant a flower, light a candle, or gaze into the sunrise/sunset or stars. These simplistic offerings, performed in humility and reverence, can change your outlook.

The practices for connecting to your Soul Voice in the realm of coaching and therapy are slightly difficult to explain, as it's ethereal and unique to each person. The mode of travel I use on this path includes dream work and interpretation. We also employ myth metaphor to reveal powerful messages. You may feel called to a certain myth or texts of ancient wisdom traditions. Study, listen to the whispers, and follow your intuition—it will guide you to these ancient wisdoms, which will connect you to your Soul Voice.

Some clients gravitate to a particular form of communication that their voices prefer to "speak" with. My client Jo is like this. She has vivid, detailed images that appear in our sessions and her dreams. Her Soul Voice comes through loud and clear.

In one particularly intriguing session, Jo showed up and related that she had accidentally left candles burning on her prayer alter when she went to work earlier that week. . There was a fire. The thought-provoking outcome was: the fire only burnt a small area above the shelf. The whole house could've burnt down but did not. We agreed we needed to dig deeper for the real meaning of this scary event.

We used Metaphor Work, in which Jo received messages from items on her sacred alter. She had a gratitude candle there. I asked her to describe the candle.

JO: "Transformed (since it had melted and burned), light, and sad."

ME: "What is the purpose of the candle?"

JO: "It is a symbol of transformation."

71

I asked the message of the candle for Jo and received, "Everything is constantly evolving and transforming. You need to remember this and not get attached to outcomes."

ME: "Where in your life do you feel transformed, light, and sad?"

JO: "In my business. With my husband away from the business, I feel a bit sad."

ME: "Can you see how the message and purpose from the candle fit into this situation in your business?"

JO: "Absolutely. I have to make decisions that are transforming me, but I need to stay unattached, and that has been really hard. Now I can understand that it's all evolving, and I don't need to hold on so tightly to old ways and patterns."

When you use the practices and exercises detailed in this book, you will begin to clear out a multitude of "noise" in your life and psyche. This will give you room to hear all of your voices. The Soul Voice will speak in both soft and loud tones, because the reception is clear and available. Hopefully, you won't have to create a "fire" in order to listen.

One day, I left the house to go grocery shopping. I wanted to listen to a podcast while doing my errands, so I was messing around on my phone trying to find the "right" talk. I felt a little anxiety (soft fear), because I was driving and shouldn't be on the phone. Fear says, "Take action," so I pressed play on the first talk that showed up.

One of the first things the speaker said was something about Judeo-Christianity. I thought, "I really don't want to listen to this." But, I was driving and needed to stay alive, so I listened. That particular podcast changed my life. It was an interview with Celtic poet and author John O'Donohue. I had never heard of him. The interview had me heart struck and body warmed for the next ninety minutes. I bought his books and Anam Cara: A Book of Celtic Wisdom *is a part of my being today.*

Anam Cara *has given me back my ancestral connection to Celtic Wisdom. I am a mystic to my core, and I love my earthy creature and plant family. Much of the time, I feel I was born into the wrong era.* Anam Cara *gives me comfort in my connection to earth and freedom in my solitude. The description of aging in the book brought me much solace in a world that values outer glamour above realness and true beauty. Through this gentle guidance of my Soul Voice—"You should listen to this podcast."—I have tapped into a new freedom. I share it often with my clients, as I frequently open up the book to whatever page is called for. The message is always related to what the client needs and is profound in its delivery.*

Joy

"Joy seems to come forth during moments of communion with nature, love and beauty—when you feel as if you're one with everything."—Karla McLaren

This expansive emotion seems to fit better in this chapter on the Soul Voice, as its message is "gratitude for the radiant moment."

Joy, like happiness and linear spirituality, can be treated as a goal to reach for and grasp onto instead of letting it arrive as a gift and a surprise. It comes softly upon you when you are present with all of your body and emotions.

You have a soul story of your own to write. It includes all of you, your problems and your past. It brings your perceived flaws to the party as strengths and personality. You did not get out of the ravages of addiction to fall prey to the goblins and dream-stealers of "problems." These challenges are the sweets of life wrapped in ugly packages and disguised as issues so that you can unwrap them, look beyond appearances, and make nectar. Your story is braver beyond what you've ever imagined, because you dare to question and connect and believe in something bigger than you: that gives you challenges to prevent you from disconnecting and playing small.

This tribe of souls *is* different, and I wouldn't have it any other way—even though it is hard a lot of the time. We get to be blessed by fire and adversity. It is as if we are purified by this fire, and in the Yogic traditions of the *yamas* and *niyamas*, this fiery blessing is called *tapas*. We build heat through our practices and challenges to burn off that ugly wrapping.

You have been chosen as part of this warrior tribe. Make space, inquire mindfully, join us in solitude, and listen carefully for Magic Key #4—the whisper of your Soul Voice.

Trauma disconnects us from Source. We have a hard time getting that connection back when we are little people with no guidance from our big people. Sobriety helps us reconnect. But, many people don't learn how to do so. They are stuck in cycling from one new addiction pattern to the next. Or, it can take years to establish an association to our own Soul Voice and guidance system. I believe with all the fibers of my being that Grounding and Boundaries practices, chakra work, and the Magic Keys in this book will give you the restfulness that one finds when partnering with all of their voices.

Exercise

Use your Grounding and Boundaries practice to prepare for this exercise. Then inquire of your image, object, dream, or vision. Describe the object with three adjectives. Now "become" the object. Take your time until you can fully "be" there. Ask the item, "What is your purpose in my life?" Make sure to write down your answer. Become the object again and ask, "What is your message for me?" When you have your answer, write it down. Return to yourself. Ask or write, "Where in my life am I the three adjectives that I used to describe the image? Then, with open mind and heart, insert the purpose and message you received into this part of your life. I am guessing you will be enthralled with your message. Be sure to thank your Soul Voice and yourself for the information.

I realize this exercise can be a bit confusing to the solo practitioner. I do recommend consulting a professional for this. I would be happy to assist you with this process. I wanted to include it, no matter the difficulty, so you would have a better idea of the process. Mystery is good, but I'm not trying to hide anything from you.

Well, that's it. You now have all the necessary tools and Magic Keys you will need for your journey. You should understand by now that this does not mean "problem free." It just means you are able to handle problems with greater stability, understanding, and intention.

Let's travel deeper into some of those areas of life most well-known for knocking us off of our foundation, shall we?

Chapter Eight—Money Honey

No conversation about healing, wholeness, problems, addiction, and you is complete without talking about money. Let's face it—money is a problem for the majority of people with addiction problems. It may or may not be one of your go to addictions or distractions. Maybe a gambling or shopping addiction was what brought you to your rock bottom. Maybe you woke up in enormous debt one day and decided to change.

There are many types of sobriety, and financial sobriety is an important topic for all of us.

My guess is that the majority of people who are in discovery don't show up with loads of money and a lack of money problems. This is because money is us and we are money.

"Show me the condition of a person's purse or wallet and I will tell you their money story."—Meadow Devor

Is the wallet torn, unorganized with papers falling out, and they can't find anything? Do they have twenty credit cards in there? Or, is it neat and tidy with the bills all facing the same way? There is something to this observation. If you are having problems with money, what does your wallet say about you and your money story? What does your bank account say? What do your income and debt say?

When I got sober, one of the first things I began to do was take a keen, honest look at what sort of game I had been playing with money. In the beginning, this was *not* fun. There are times when it still is neither pleasant nor one of my favorite activities. It's one of the main reasons for writing this chapter. Even though, each year, my financial situation gets better in some ways, in other ways it got worse. I was conscious and aware of where my money was going and what I was doing with it, yet one giant debt after another would pop up. It didn't seem to matter how hard I tried or how much I saved—I couldn't get ahead of the game. My parents keep lifting me. While I am committed to making good on their assistance, at times I wonder if it keeps me from maturing. Or, maybe it is so I can do the hard things my Soul Voice keeps guiding me to do.

I always thought that the way my father was able to show love was by giving me a loan instead of a hug. Then I realized that by receiving the loan, I felt loved. This money stuff can be messy, complicated, and intertwined with all sorts of crazy meanings and realizations.

Money work is spiritual work. It is "love yourself, take care of yourself" work.

Basic Principles of Money

There are some basic principles of money that, if you follow, can help you establish a foundation and a feeling of a little more friendship with money. You are probably not going to want to follow these principles, but if you do and you are consistent, you can begin to transform your money story.

- **Track your income.** You have to know where you are coming from to know where you are going. Write it down. Especially if you are self-employed or make cash for the majority of your income. If you are a tipped employee or self-employed, you will need to track your income longer than someone who receives regular paychecks so that you can establish an average monthly income.

- **Track what you spend.** Write this down too. Yes, even that little snack or the late night movie binge on Hulu. This is a real eye-opener in many ways. You will see where you spend money, and this shows you what is important to you. I like good food and concerts rather than a fancy car or the latest fashions. You will find out where you spend money that you could be saving, such as buying nice coffee and brewing at home instead of that daily five dollar latte. Don't censor or pick on yourself while you are doing this. All you are doing is becoming aware.

- Take the time you need to establish your **baseline income and out flow**. Don't procrastinate, but don't rush either. Dave Ramsey's Financial Peace University Program is brilliant for helping you establish a new money story. And he's really funny, which makes it easy to want to learn. The following ideas and tips are from his program. To go deeper, find Dave at financialpeaceuniversity.com.

- After establishing your foundation, you will want to **create a budget.** Spend all your money on paper before you actually spend it. Write it down! I have all of my written budgets from the last five years, just so I can look at them and see how far I've come. This process is fluid and changes as you change (see the relationship?).

- **Create an emergency fund** of $1,000. Sell stuff, work a second or third job, and eat at home. Tell your friends that until you get this fund established you aren't buying things you don't need.

- **Save 10 percent, and give away 10 percent.** I found this much easier to do when I broke it down to small chunks. For example: If I make $100, I put $10 in a savings envelope and $10 in a "give away" envelope. At the end of the month, I can put my savings in an account, and I give away the other to somewhere that makes me feel happy by the work they do in the world. For some people this is church—for others it is helping a friend or organization that always makes you smile. This 10 percent principle is an ancient one. It is life transforming. If you can't start with 10 percent, start with 5 percent. Please just start. You will be amazed at how you suddenly seem to always have money when you need it.

- **Only spend the money you have.** The number of people living beyond their means in our country is scary. In just a few generations, we have gone from saving to be able to have and do things, to living in extreme amounts of debt so we can indulge our addictions on every level. Cut up your credit cards, get that emergency fund in place, and become someone with true financial sobriety.

- To pay off debt, **create a debt snowball**. Make a list of your debts. Pay off the smallest first, so you can feel successful—this will be your largest payment. For everything else, make minimum payments. You may need to make phone calls to discuss arrangements. Once you pay off the smallest debt, move on to the next one and pay it. The energy you create by crossing these debts off magically makes things happen (like a raise or a new higher paying job), which in turn allows you to pay off your debt faster.

Finances can be a really tough conversation. I avoided this conversation most of my life. Financial sobriety brought me closer to telling the truth to myself about money, but not all of the way. I had to have a couple more lessons before I could even begin to admit all the ways I use money (or the lack thereof) to play small and not step up to my life's purpose. I had to come to the decision that staying where I was (not being able to take vacations I wanted to, still having large amounts of debt, living in fear, etc.) was more painful than working a little bit harder and telling the truth even more. I have found that structure, budgeting, and living within my means is more enjoyable and rewarding than I had anticipated.

Money may be one of the ways in which you have to

put on your big-person pants more than any other. Repairing your relationship with money will help you repair your relationship with yourself and others. If you can't trust money, why would you trust yourself with money? How can you trust others? How can you trust life?

Before I leave you with these practices to ponder, we need to have a conversation about using money as avoidance or distraction. Guess what? It's just like alcohol or sex or sugar.

The more obvious ways this avoidance plays out is when you feel bad and go shopping to avoid feeling the feelings. You can be sober and still stuck in the trap of needing to have "things" to make your life look pretty on the outside, in hopes that you or anyone else won't notice how icky you feel on the inside. A super creative way to do this is buying the latest yoga retreat (you can't afford), because it will "fix all your problems." It seems and feels legit, and just about everyone will support you in this sort of choice, because it's for "spiritual and personal growth and healing."

On the flip side, you can be cruising along and growing in sobriety, paying off your debt and saving money. Things are looking good, and yet you are not fulfilling your destiny (you feel restless and unfulfilled). The universe gives you a great big push out of your comfortable nest (financial difficulty), and now you don't even know how you are going to pay that debt commitment let alone your bills. Angela Lauria calls this a "wanting problem." You keep *wanting* to be out of debt and have more money, yet you aren't truly willing to do the work to make this happen. You have an amazing excuse for it not happening: "I don't have the money." Ugh! It's like wanting to lose weight yet not going to the gym or not ceasing to eat ice cream every night. Then when you don't get the job or the relationship you want, you get to say, "It's because I'm fat."

Isolation plays into the mix as well. As a species, we are going faster and faster, becoming more and more addicted, buying shinier and shinier things to fill the void created by our disconnection from each other. We could slow down and invite friends over for a home-cooked meal instead of dining out. We could go for walks and play games instead of buying the latest app that tricks you into thinking you have friends. What about attending a play or a concert with loved ones and creating artful memories instead of buying Christmas presents that cause you to overspend? What about really looking at each other over a cup of tea instead of meeting at the bar to shut down our emotions while we are together?

"How do we start to rebuild a society where we don't feel so alone and afraid, and where we can form healthier bonds? How do we build a society where we look for happiness in one another rather than in consumption?"—Johann Hari

How do we build our own internal resources and find happiness from within rather than grasping for straws from the external world?

Exercise

Money stuff is foundational, so we want to work with the root chakra. You may want to re-read that section before this exercise. In order to understand your money story, you have to tell the truth. Start with yourself. You *can* begin to ask the hard questions of yourself. Make sure you have your journal at hand so that you can track your answers.

Start with your Grounding and Boundaries practice. Then bring your awareness to the root chakra area. Imagine the color red at the tip of your tailbone and let that red expand down into the earth, coloring your grounding cord. You can remain in a comfortable seated position (on the floor or in a chair with your feet on the ground). Even better, fold at the waist over some stacked blankets or pillows. Let yourself feel supported by these simple props and the contact of earth energy. Take your time and ask the following questions.

Money is_____.

Do I have a lot of money? Why or why not?

What is the story I have about money right now?

What is my biggest fear about money?

What is my biggest hope about money?

What am I afraid of?

Am I more comfortable here in my problem than doing some "adulting" and going to work?

This exercise, done with compassion and intention, should be very revealing. Take some time at the end of each session to restore yourself inside your boundary. Honor and thank all of your voices as well.

Please remember to be kind to yourself. You may get through just one or two of these questions at a time. That's perfectly fine. It's highly likely you were not taught any of these ways to inquire into yourself and how you operate in the world. Just the fact that you are sober and willing to look deeper and grow gives you bad ass, warrior status. Remember to use all of your Magic Keys. Get support. Take baby steps. Remember to use the circular path instead of linear thinking. And let the miracles begin to unfold.

Chapter Nine—Healing Trauma

"The question is not 'why the addiction?' The question is 'why' the pain?"—Dr. Gabor Maté

I have often wondered, "Why me?" I had a childhood of love and comfort, play and adventure. Why did I delve into full-blown disordered eating and addiction? My family members did not go through this, and they had the same childhood I did.

I believe the answer lies in the disconnection theory of addiction. Past and recent ground-breaking studies (which, by the way, have been underfunded and not made headlines) show that humans and animals—when isolated, neglected, and traumatized—will become addicted to blunt the pain of their existence. These same humans and animals—when surrounded by companions, love, food, and play—will go through withdrawals from their substance addictions but will no longer "pick-up."

My mother, when she found out she was pregnant with me, experienced extreme shame and guilt. She had three choices: marry a man she hardly knew, get sent to the country and give up her baby, or become "that" woman. She chose to give up a job she loved, move, marry my father, and embark upon a story built on a lie. She felt embarrassed and very unhappy, all the while pasting a smile on her face and pretending to be "in love." She gained all of thirteen pounds during the pregnancy, as she was intensely ill. I came into a world that already *felt like a trap. I was independent and defiant.*

I was shamed as a child and grew up never feeling quite "good enough." I just did not feel I could do anything right to please my father. I retreated into books, horseback riding, my (quite creative) imagination, and being outdoors.

When I was eleven, my parents divorced. We moved. My cat got sick and died, and I also became terribly ill. All of these events occurred within a short time period. I further retreated into the safety zone of reading.

We moved again. I now had two new homes in places where I didn't know anyone, and I again felt alone and like I didn't measure up.

By the time I was thirteen I was using the warmth of alcohol and the buzz of diet pills to belong somewhere. I began to "fit in" with the party crowd, and being skinny became an obsession.

Defiant behavior was my go-to survival technique. Underneath all of this apparent "belonging," I always felt ashamed. I really did want to be good and be loved and do great things. Yet, I was already out of control with patterns and behaviors I had no idea how to manage. This lifestyle would continue in one form or another for the next thirty-five years. I waitressed and bartended and played and partied. This, I was good at. At one point I went to an out-patient rehab for cocaine use and left having switched to methamphetamines. I continued my disordered eating until I was forty-one. I was thrown in jail for DUI's and driving on suspended licenses. My relationships turned into disasters, as my addictions controlled most of my actions.

I tell you this story to highlight the trauma and shame that kept being further driven into my body and psyche. It was always present, and I was always trying something to make the horrible feelings go away. Chiropractic College and owning a business in many ways further traumatized me. I had no way out. I could stop, but I couldn't stay stopped.

Addiction, failure, and heartbreak brought me to my knees. I finally couldn't go another second feeling how I felt. I chose sobriety on February 3, 2013.

Life got better. After three months, I made my way to AA. That helped too. I worked the steps, made amends, and (my favorite part) had sober friends. But I had not healed my trauma. I still felt lost, confused, and alone much of the time. I needed guidance beyond a sponsor. I needed someone who had been through what I had and was also educated in body-centered methods. I needed something beyond talk! You are holding and reading what I needed.

Addiction of any kind becomes the savior for those who have been traumatized. Remember that trauma does not have to be one significant event or abuse. Small abuses over time—things like working in the emergency room or in war zones—can cause a person to become a victim of trauma. There is birth trauma and injury trauma. There is the trauma of neglect and the trauma of rape. There is emotional trauma and mental trauma. All of them cause one to seek out relief of the pain. When a person is traumatized and then turns to a substance or behavior to ease the hurt, our culture doesn't readily turn to us in compassion. Instead, we heap shame upon the user, which then causes further trauma. Jails, institutions, violence, and poverty await the hardcore addicts, which drives the shame deeper still. When one looks upon the landscape of addiction from this angle, you might ask, "Why *wouldn't* they use whatever they can to stop the torment?"

Addicts shame other addicts. I've done it. I've felt it. We turn away from our own in fear and disgust. It's as if we can't handle looking at someone still acting out our own agony. We have to distance ourselves from that disease.

When you experience trauma of any kind and do not have the tools to respond, the beautiful thing that the human psyche does is disconnect so that you can handle the trauma and survive. This physiological response is so fine-tuned—you may not even remember the event.

All of your voices are involved in the experience of trauma. It's probably apparent to you that your Soul Voice would be involved in the healing of trauma, but what about the other voices? This is the beauty of this unique work: all of your voices get to come to the party and support you in becoming uniquely you—scarred, maybe battle weary for the moment, and on the mend.

Magic Keys and Healing Trauma

Grounding and Boundaries practice along with chakra work is very, very important in supporting yourself when you begin to work on problems of disconnection, disassociation, and trauma. This ability to disassociate is why we need to use the tools in this book—so we can break the pattern of leaving ourselves.

Mind Voice

Your Mind Voice is probably not the most skilled voice to use in healing from traumatic situations. That being said, Thought Work and the resulting turn-arounds can be very helpful in understanding better that all humans are just that: human. We are flawed, abused, stupid, mean, violent, and horrible. But, we aren't all of those things all of the time.

Your Mind Voice can help you find the proper resources needed to help you help yourself. The mind can be a tricky place, as it really believes it is protecting you. It may try to tell you not to proceed with your new knowledge and Magic Key superpowers. It will try to keep you stuck in the old familiar states and places, i.e. problems. Using Thought Work on those kinds of thoughts—such as, "I can't. I'm not good enough—who am I to try to change?"—is very revealing. Thought Work can also be of assistance when you are falling into blaming others.

Heart Voice

Your Heart Voice is one of the best ways to work with disconnection and trauma. Emotions that are honored, felt, and paid attention to can bring you to the threshold of your pain—then they take you past that pain, building a bridge to carry you to the sweet rest of forgiveness and release.

You now have the tools to listen to the messages of your emotions. You can ask the questions for anger or sadness and then wait for the answer. Emotions are meant to be noticed, felt, and listened to. Then they can go on their way until the next time you need their message. Becoming proficient at working with your feelings is a skill. You may be very creative at not feeling your feelings. You may be a master at avoiding your feelings. Or, maybe you are able to welcome your emotions as friends—because you didn't feel anything for so long—but you have no idea what to do about them. This was definitely how I was after embarking on my sober journey. I was so happy to feel something, but I did not like feeling hijacked or overwhelmed by my feelings. So I distracted, avoided, and came up with new addictions in order to self soothe.

I still do this. So will you. And, you will get better and better at noticing when you are distracting and avoiding your feelings.

Body Voice

The Body Voice is the most profound of all the voices

when it comes to working with trauma patterns. Remembering that the body carries everything that ever happened to you might sound scary, but your body is your home. It wants you to live here, in the body. It wants you to listen to its messages, and if you don't, it may start to give you gifts in really funnily wrapped packages, like pain and illnesses. Treating your body like the animal it is can help you unwrap these packages in a kind, gentle way. It's like comforting a scared, cold shelter dog. Holding your body, wrapping it up in warm blankets, telling it you love it and you are here to listen to it will transmute your relationship to your trauma.

When you are experiencing pain, tension or an illness symptom, get quiet with your eyes closed, and place your hands on the affected area. Ask it questions like, "Who are you? What do you want? What do you need from me?" Take your time.

As with all of these keys, you may think that you are crazy or that this is not working, but it is! The answers will be the first images, sensations, memories, or thoughts that appear. Having a conversation with your body might be the most magical of all the tools shared in this book. Your little animal will share with you things you never dreamed were possible. Take the time to nurture your relationship with your body and listen to its needs.

When you ask what it needs and receive an answer, please do that thing. You may need to write a forgiveness note or get a massage. Maybe you just need to say, "I'm sorry," to it. It might call for a warm blanket or a bath. You can treat these requests like a magic potion, pouring the potion into your body. If you have a lifetime of abuse toward your body, this new relationship may take some time and a lot of cultivation. Again—just like the poor scared pup—patience, compassion, and love are what are called for here.

The Body Keeps the Score by Bessel Van Der Kolk, M.D. is one of the most comprehensive texts on how the brain, mind, emotions, and body respond and react to trauma. It is a fascinating and brilliant read. As you delve deeper into your relationship with yourself and your "animal," you may want to gather more information on how you can better understand why you do what you do.

This piece of the puzzle in particular is unique to the type of coaching work I and my colleagues are trained to do. It is one of the main reasons body-centered recovery coaching works so well, helping you to uncover what has been keeping you stuck in old patterns and problems.

Soul Voice

Your Soul Voice is the voice that kept you alive with a shrouded flame of hope and determination, which you quite possibly kept hidden from yourself. It is why you made it through your addiction. This voice is the whisper that keeps nudging you to learn more, practice more, and just be. It supports you in surrendering to your very unique and beautiful path that, even though looks like just problems, is glistening with the diamonds of your tears.

Beauty Heals

Throughout the accounting of history, beauty heals. This beauty is the beauty of nature, not man-made glamour and impossible standards as another commodity to be sold. Broken, bloodied warriors watch the pinks and oranges of the sunset color the sky and breathe deep, filling their hearts with relief at the end of a battle well fought. Wise men and women of the ancients peered into the flames of fires and brought back messages of hope.

Flowers have long been admired for their delicate sunny faces and scents of a new day, love, or uplifting of a sad heart. Walking the forest trails, breathing the scents of trees, feeling the cushion of pine needles and mulch beneath the feet brings one to realize the sacred connection with nature. Watching, caring for, and loving animals bring a fascination with earthlings—we will never really understand their wildness and mystery. It is precisely this unknown that brings us such curiosity and solace when we surround ourselves with wild things.

When you find yourself with problem after problem, you must immerse yourself as much as possible in connecting with beauty that is not human. Get your face away from the phone, computer, and television. Go outdoors. Feel the sand on your feet, swim in the ocean, walk or run the dirt trails. Play with animals. Pet them, love on them, and allow yourself to be loved upon. We are at a threshold of destroying our own animal natures, as most of humanity has almost completely disconnected from the healing of nature. We have forgotten the importance of quiet and solitude. We *need* to feel the wind and sun on our skin, to touch rocks and trees. We need to wade through streams instead of surf the web.

Music is also another fascinating way to heal your psyche from unresolved trauma. Celtic and classical music, songs that touch the heart and soul, are fabulous additions to any journey toward a life of meaning and purpose.

Pack up your adventurer's tool kit along with your Magic Keys, and go explore the part of you that belongs to the earth. Even if you can only see the glory of the in-between times of twilight, sunrise, and sunset—do that. It's something.

Kind, Compassionate Reason

As trauma, shame, and isolation cause one to turn to the solace of addiction—empathy, connection, and compassion heal addiction.

I believe this is one of the many reasons twelve-step programs do work. Suddenly you are surrounded by people who understand you, smile at you, and accept you. You have a group of friends, where before you were so very alone. You are connected with others in study, laughter, and play. This soothes the ache.

This is connection from the outside in and comes highly recommended. The tools in this book, however, work from the inside out. And these tools will give you the ultimate fellowship, one that cannot be taken from you: the friendship of you.

Do remember that for everything you have done and for everything you do that you may not understand or like, there is a kind compassionate reason. You have been doing the very best with what you have, and that is something. While traveling on your journey, through the peaks and the valleys, you have been learning new things and trying new ideas. You are meeting new people and new parts of yourself. You have been welcoming the mystery of life, even when you have been afraid. You are guided and protected by light.

This path, this adventure, is not for the timid. But it is *totally* worth it.

Putting It All Together

Initially, when I begin to work with people, I introduce Grounding and Boundaries and chakra work first. Afterward, I show clients the Four Voices during four different sessions. Each person and their story are unique. I do not know ahead of time which voice is going to come forward to give their particular message. Sessions are always uncommon in their particular individuality. They are like a meandering stream that leads to a stunning waterfall or lakeside.

Later, as the client becomes more skilled, trusting and committed to doing their part, I can begin to combine techniques and intuition. More nuances are revealed as each person peels off layers of protection and survival tactics they no longer need to navigate their inner and outer worlds.

It is because of this combination of unique alchemy that I struggle to create an exercise for you here. It's something that comes to light with space and over time. I know that if you are patient and keep using these foundations and Magic Keys, you can discover much on your own. And, to be completely transparent, it can be extremely difficult. As humans heal trauma, it is highly recommended, supportive, and beneficial to have a guide who has traveled before you.

As you explore, trust this book as a map. Use it as a guidebook written by the guide. Just know it has its limitations, as maps inherently do. I'm doing my best to lead you through the dangers and pitfalls without being right there with you.

Chapter Ten—Adventurers and Relationships

"Your task is not to seek for love, but to seek and find all the barriers within yourself that you have built against it."—A Course in Miracles

- Grounding and Boundaries
- Chakra Work
- Mind Voice
- Body Voice
- Emotion Voice
- Soul Voice

We have covered a lot of ground to get to this place on our journey. You will be glad for the insight and wisdom you now carry with you. I daresay, you will need all of the tools all of the time to navigate relationship territory. I don't think I would be far off if I said that relationships are the beginning and end of all our addictions.

Think about it. We are in relationship to the earth, whether we notice or not. We are born through and because of a relationship of some sort, which brought our parents together. We are in a relationship from that point on with those parents and grandparents, siblings and so on, even if we never see them again. We are in relationships with friends, neighbors, and teachers. We have relationships with animals, co-workers, children, partners, and spouses.

We have fleeting relationships with flight attendants, customers, and the person across from you at the stop light. We have cyber-space relationships with people we have never physically met. We have best friend relationships and long-distance relationships.

Each relationship is unique. Some you will never think about again and others will impact you for your entire lifetime.

And if we continue on with the trauma theory as a major component of addiction, that gives insight into how relationships (or lack thereof) are fundamentally related to addiction. Relationships bring us our greatest joy and our most exquisite agony.

If you became addicted to chase away a pain, it is highly likely that pain came from some sort of relationship trauma.

Zena was just a baby when her formative relationship with her parents went awry. She spent almost twenty years of numbing herself to forget that pain. The death of her sister drove the pain deeper and she came near to doing the same thing to herself.

Lilly was emotionally abused and neglected by her parents. She was also sexually abused by her step-brother and hospitalized for anorexia. She continued the abusive and addictive behavior patterns and repeated them by marrying an emotionally distant and abusive man.

Melecia parented herself and her sister. She uses

work, isolation, and procrastination to avoid romantic relationships altogether. She creates reasons to overeat and distract herself from her true passions.

Jo's childhood was fraught with the anxiety of a dangerously alcoholic mother and the requirements of living up to impossible standards of perfection. Her descent into alcoholism and isolation was fast and hard. Committed relationships eluded her throughout early adulthood.

Lisa wasn't taught to empower herself. Her mother was overbearing and critical. Lisa drank to feel a source of freedom from being smothered. Her familial and romantic relationships all suffered from this pattern.

My patterns involved circumstances surrounding my birth and later my parents' divorce, moving, illness, and the loss of my cat. Each relationship that I didn't know how to handle (and the subsequent loss) drove my trauma deeper. Until just recently, romantic relationships tended to baffle me still. I find solace with animals, family, and close friends.

Can you see where I am going with this? Problematic relationships tend to be more the rule and less the exception for those of us with stories of addictions.

Because we as a species are interconnected with each other and life, we need to be more subtle and nuanced in our dealings with each other. We need each other so much. Yet, it seems our world is headed in the other direction.

"[Maybe] the opposite of addiction isn't sobriety. It's connection."—Johann Hari

How Do We Do It?

In all transparency, this chapter has been the hardest for me to write. I do not feel I have great heaps wisdom to offer you. But I do have some.

Solitude

Do this. Spend time alone. Use this time to get to know and love yourself deeply, just as you are. This is solitude not isolation, and it has been one of my greatest sources of joy in the past few years of sobriety.

Solitude enables me to listen to my Four Voices and to see my path in a clearer manner. I've always had a better time with animals as best friends than humans. Surprisingly, I enjoy feeling very close to my friends and family—we collaborate in love, play, work and laughter, easily and almost effortlessly.

The tale of the solitary adventurer is not a rare one. The solo hero often requires and seeks out solitude. Relationships tend to baffle and disturb the lone traveler. When they do reach "civilization," they often run into trouble. Avoidance works for this one, as it keeps them out of painful interactions. Always in these epic journeys, our hero finds companions along the way—friendships that connect and deepen through shared trials and dangerous mountain paths.

Romantic Relationships

Quite honestly, I want to skip this part altogether. Society has taught me the goal is to have a long-term relationship. I don't know if this really is healthy or not for everyone. Is it cultural conditioning or what we are driven to do as a species?

I do know I can question my thoughts and beliefs around this topic, and that is a comforting practice for me. The longest romantic/intimate relationship I had was the "best" one, and we were together for four years. It pretty much ended while I was getting sober and was a catalyst to stop my addictive behavior. Dissolving this partnership also almost wrecked me. It's a miracle I didn't return to numbing the pain with drugs and alcohol.

It's taken me most of my sobriety to date again (not that I'm not interested). I fumble around and learn more about myself each time, and then I try again. I'm still sorting how to best handle those types of friendships, and I remain convinced that I would like to try being in a committed long-term relationship as long as we didn't live together full time. I'm not sure if I would get an A in relationship school were I to live with my partner.

I lean upon all of the practices in this book religiously to help myself make sense of whom and what show up in my life. I suspect that the outcome of all of this practice in relationships is for me to learn that *I am the greatest love of my life.*

Even so, there are times when I yearn for a person in man form that totally "gets me."

With all of that being said, I look at couples who have been together for eons and wonder, "Can I do that? Do I even want to?" What I am doing now is preparing for love. I am stable enough in my practices that I've come to a place where I can dream again. I am working with my coach to uncover and release the barriers I have built against love.

Wherever you find yourself in romantic relationships, I do know that the Grounding and Boundaries practices and Magic Keys will only enhance your ability to take care of yourself, love yourself, not lose yourself, and to stay on your own mat.

Family

I have been privileged to watch my colleagues and my clients heal their familial wounds in profound manners using the tools in this book. I connected up with my family, forgave them, had real conversations, and even played with them. Considering there was a time when I purposely lived out-of-state from them, this is great progress. Each thought, each emotion, and each body message clears the path for greater love and connection. Heck, sometimes they even ask me for advice.

I believe your Soul Voice will come through for you here and will give you much guidance as you make your way to greater self-understanding. Remember: it is not a race, and you are divinely guided.

Friendships and Connection

Hey, do this too!

Make some friends. Be real. Be vulnerable—it's the new strong. Reach out your hand to someone that looks like they may be hurting more than you.

You can mentor someone with a talent that you have. Ask people to do things. Go to talks and yoga and music gatherings.

Go to some meetings and meet people. The Fellowship of AA has been a steady force in my sober life. I have sober friends, and that feels really good.

By now, you are quite used to my advice of using Grounding and Boundaries for, well, everything! These tools are in your adventurers pack for a reason. Use them and use them wisely. You can even use them as a way to connect with others. What a great topic for an interesting conversation.

So here we are at the end of addiction. Again, what if the opposite of addiction is not sobriety but connection?

I am definitely not advocating that you start numbing out and distracting with your old patterns. I am suggesting that you keep inquiring as to how you can continuously connect with yourself and others, so you don't isolate and shut down.

Zena's five year relationship (that was on the rocks when she began working with me) is now thriving! They actually communicate and appreciate each other. As she is able to open up and become more vulnerable, he shows up as well. No matter what happens, they are in agreement that their time together has enhanced each other's lives.

Lilly spends more time working with strengthening her boundaries and grounding so that she can feel safe without the input of others. She makes conscious choices even if they are difficult ones, like staying in an unhappy relationship. As she continues these practices, maybe this relationship will also transform.

Melecia has revived her love of dance and moving her body. She feels much better and more like herself as she rekindles her passions. She too may find that she is the "love of her life." We have begun preparing her for love and uncovering the barriers she has built against it.

Jo is married. They have a relationship built upon communication and a foundation of each working to be the best they can be. They own a business together, in which she must use skilled tools of connection and community.

Lisa is single-handedly transforming the family history of co-dependency and addiction as she sets her boundaries in a compassionate manner. She is modeling behavior they much needed. This will change the story of her lineage in subtle yet profound ways.

Then, there is me. I'm getting my toes wet by making sure I go do new things and meet new people. I work on expressing my emotions and feelings rather than just coming from an intellectual perspective. I work on *"loving my people" for who they are. I can more easily sit with people while they are having hardships . . . this is a huge gift for all of us.*

Some adventure stories have happy fantasy endings, but not many. What we have here are real stories of lives in luminous stages of transformation and connection. We have lives of addiction being healed by personal responsibility.

Anam Cara

John O'Donohue's book *Anam Cara* gives us the gift of the concept of "soul friends." Anam cara means "soul friend."

With the anam cara you could share your innermost self, your mind and your heart. This friendship was an act of recognition and belonging. When you had an anam cara your friendship cut across all convention, morality and category. You were joined in an ancient and eternal way with the "friend of your soul." The Celtic understanding did not set limitations of space or time on the soul."—John O'Donahue

My life has been blessed with a few friends of my soul. Some of them have been animal friends. This soul light, these people of my tribe can be distant for months or years, yet the minute we speak it is as if no time has passed. We hold each other in kind regard whether we speak often or not, whether we reside nearby or not. Anam cara will be there through your troubled times to support and hold you. They will laugh with you in the best of times and give their wisdom freely and kindly. This friendship can and will heal your very being. I wish for you the beauty of the anam cara. Just as you let the soul come to you, let your friends of the soul show up in your life. As *you* show up for you, so will they.

Putting It All Together

You will need to follow your voices and your own guidance system as you maneuver relationship territory. It's a wonderful opportunity for you to use the Magic Keys that (again) I wish I would've had. There is always room to change and grow and have revelations along the way.

Speaking of, the next chapter is all about being prepared for the obstacles you are sure to run into. Let's take a fair look into your future so you can avoid some nasty surprises, shall we?

Chapter Eleven—The Way of the Sober Warrior

"It's a dangerous business Frodo, going out of your door. You step onto the Road and if you don't keep your feet, there is no knowing where you might be swept off to."— The Hobbit

Dear Adventurer,

You have come so far and been so brave on this journey. You have embraced each Magic Key and have unlocked many doors. I know this hasn't been easy. You are almost home where you can rest for a bit and recharge. You will get to bask in the contentment of a job well done.

I have news for you. You will soon be asked to travel again. In the famous words of hobbit Bilbo Baggins, "I want to see mountains again, mountains, Gandalf." You will want to grow and expand and learn more about yourself and your world. Quite likely, this growth will look like problems. Sooner rather than later, you will recognize them for what they are, growth opportunities and you will reach in your adventurer's knapsack for the appropriate key and scale the mountain.

I wish you grace,

Layne

The road has been long. I know it continues ever on. I must have known on some level that sobriety was going to be hard, because I avoided this route for many, many years. The way can be painful. It just isn't quite as painful as the sickness that addiction brings.

I arrived at the beginning of my sobriety with some tools. I was given others in AA. I use them all. The practices and keys in this book are magical to me and I use them daily.

This journey contains mountains to climb, pitfalls to avoid, and bridges you must build. Adventurers usually have some sort of inkling about the obstacles they may face. What follows is an accounting of the bogs and marshes to avoid if you can.

Addiction Transfer

If you don't explore *why* you drank or drugged or whatever it is for you in the first place, you won't know what feelings and thoughts you have been trying to ignore. And instead, you will find a very creative new way to distract yourself.

You might try Netflix binges, coffee, getting into new (quite possibly harmful) relationships, blaming, gambling, smoking, a new drug, eating, over-exercising, complete disassociation, shopping, and/or something else not listed to distract yourself from all the feelings coming up that you didn't address.

You may find yourself fairly far along on your sobriety

path and notice that new hooks and distractions keep showing up. Or, you might not notice, but then a new hardship shows up, which reveals your distraction or new addiction pattern.

These "rocks in the path" are more "gifts in funny packages" to ask you to slow down and find out what you are avoiding. Do you reach for a cigarette whenever you have a stressful or aggravating moment? Sometimes we can't even handle too much happiness, and we have to use something to tone it down.

This stuff is real, and it's time to get out your Magic Keys and ask those questions. What am I feeling and thinking that has me all upset? What am I trying to avoid? Am I grounded or completely out of my body?

Sometimes all of this feeling your feelings and doing all the work and the self-questioning and being coached and not getting addicted to other things is going to feel exhausting! Know this. Be aware of it. Get real about it. It's your way of living your best life.

You can rest. You can choose to disconnect with TV or over-exercising or whatever you choose. But, make a choice. Go into it consciously with intention. Tell yourself you are taking a much needed break from all the exploration. And then do that. With love and awareness, you will come away from your break refreshed and recharged, instead of misplaced guilt for being so hard on yourself. Remember, journeys are not taken in one day.

It's going to seem like the rest of the world, doesn't have to work as hard to just be normal and happy. Here's the deal with that: The majority of them *are* working just as hard or harder to not feel their feelings of pain, horror, fear, and sadness. It's the great human cover up.

The Fuck-Its

As a person that very creatively uses addictions to cope, you are most likely quite familiar with having a case of the "fuck-its." News flash, they happen in sobriety too. You are going to get overwhelmed, tired, and angry—generally not feel up to the task—and you are going to say, "Fuck it." You will over-eat, over-smoke, run away, and quit. You will stall out while surrounded by goblins, and you will cower and sulk. Maybe you will begin to go through your days with a mind-numbing sense of just existing.

It's wondrous to know this and be able to become conscious of it happening.

Again, the best (novice) warrior way is to have a grand case of the "fuck-its." Kick rocks, burn a big fire, put up your boundaries, shoot errant flames at the goblins, and then come back to earth. Pick up the smoldering branches, get out your Magic Keys, and get back on the path.

The greatest part is realizing that your humanity is just like everyone else's humanity—that you have guides and friends to help—and that each time you acknowledge these places of "yuck," you won't stay there as long. Soon you may even notice the signs before you get there. Maybe your body hurts in a weird new way. Maybe you are crabby and irritable for "no reason." "Aha! I'm heading into no-man's land. I need to stop, get prepared, and use my Keys."

The Spiritual Program as Perfection and Distraction

One of the reasons addicts who get sober are so brilliant is that they want so much to become better people. They are actively involved in living their lives. Sometimes this can translate to trying anything and everything to "get it right." It's like we spend so much time trying to make up for being a "shitty person" in the past and trying to make "living amends," that we forget to actually *live*.

Our spiritual growth and programs becomes a new rigorous, linear path of perfection. We forget to let life flow. We unconsciously find ourselves right back where we began—trying to control ourselves, everything, and everyone around us—and we wake up miserable with some sort of "control hangover."

This can become a dangerous place for those who have a hard time setting good boundaries, as sobriety means, "I'm trying so hard to be *nice*." They can become door mats and get walked all over by getting mixed up with being the "good little girl or boy." Spiritual sober people don't get mad or make waves, you know? All of a sudden we have some warped idea that we have to be a Buddha.

Surrendering to what life has in store for you is a

magnificent solution to this "spiritual program as perfection" problem. As you ground, question your thoughts, listen to your body and emotional messages, and follow your soul's quiet voice. This will unwrap the gift of you. Your own organic, natural spiritual life will flow forth. It won't contain "shoulds" and "have tos"— so much as an intuitive call to what absolutely feels right for you!

The soul's light that comes back on in sobriety will be the flame lighting your way when you can drop the sickly glow of perfectionism.

Goblins and Other Disguises

You will get waylaid by other people, places, and things. They will appear negative or well-meaning. You will want to blame them for everything. You *will* blame them for all of your obstacles and the creation of your problems. Acknowledge your humanness in these situations too. Feel your feelings, set up boundaries, write stuff down and when you are ready, put your adventurer pants back on and get to taking responsibility for what is yours to do. There are things that happened to you that cannot be undone. What you can do is acknowledge that these things are never going to be "OK" with you. Acknowledge that you are working through it. You can heal from even that. You cannot control other people's behavior. It's wasted time and effort. You *must* forge onward, working only on yourself. *You* are the only warrior you can change.

Life is hard. You will fall down. You will have skinned

knees and bruises. You must get back up and do the tough things anyway. It can feel daunting to be sober and feeling all the feels when its' so darn hard. Culturally, we are not taught to do this. Be aware, it is in every movie, magazine, advertisement and book—when life gets gritty, take a drink, smoke, cookie, or social media hit.

Surround yourself with other warriors doing the hard stuff of feeling, questioning, loving, and adventuring into this territory. Together, we are changing the conversation. We need you to be a part of this change. We need movies, groups, and brave people to ask the questions of "Why? What's really going on? What are you feeling?" instead of "Here, have a drink."

Don't be surprised when life feels unyielding. If you are prepared for the demons, goblins and dark places, you also get the joy and contentment of a journey well lived. The sunset is glorious over the battlefield.

Chapter Twelve—Awareness Ever After

There is no going back. Just like when Frodo Baggins wished many times that he had never offered to carry the ring to Mordor, envisioning his hearth fire merrily burning, you are too far along the path to go back.

You will come home though. I am hoping you feel more at home, right now. Waking up, making a difference in your life and the lives of others is, at times, a heavy torch to bear. At the end of the day, just like Frodo and thousands of other heroes, you will not regret bearing this light. It's the light of your heart, and this journey is absolutely one you have been meant to take.

The cool thing is, now you have these Magic Keys to assist you. They don't get old. Every time I use these techniques on myself and my clients, the information is unique to each person. Each and every session is different and special.

Getting Used to New Practices

Just as it takes time to get used to living sober, it takes time to learn to use all of your Magic Keys. Remember your guides who have gone before you and travel beside you. Take baby steps, and do what feels the best to you in each situation. Just do something—even if it's breathing, sitting in the sunlight and grounding, or writing a few lines in your journal.

As you drop your stories around each thing (I "have" to do this, "can't" do that) and listen in to what your voices are telling you, your best practices will show up where they are supposed to show up.

You won't be perfect with this, probably ever, so just get over that notion.

Note: One of the most creative ways we use to stay stuck in hard places is to "forget" to use our keys. Just ask quietly, "What do you want me to do now?" and remember the answer.

Grounding and Boundaries, chakra work, and the Four Voices will serve you on all of your journeys. They totally work if you work them. You will be able to use one or more of the keys in relationship situations, financial growth, health issues, and making decisions about well . . . anything. You have ways to question yourself that very few people utilize.

Life is full of problems. Humans have difficulties and challenges every single day. Our discomfort gets bigger when we don't understand how to handle our problems. We are sold this myth that we need these perfect, Zen-like lives, especially in sobriety. This myth damages us and makes us feel lousy about ourselves when we have rough things happen to us. I honestly feel sad for people when I watch them go through the death of loved ones and their response is, "God is good." It feels like such bullshit. Maybe they cry at home when they are alone, but wow, covering up all those feelings? Isn't that the disconnection we used when we were addicted? Doesn't that response take away from the honoring of your emotions? It certainly doesn't invite others to get close.

On the other hand, our Magic Keys don't promote wallowing or sulking. Instead, they invite honoring, awareness, and self-love. You might find yourself having a pity party when you lose your way at times. This is the brilliance of this process—it's *a process* and one you are never finished with. You get to grow yourself up, over and over. The warrior never stops training. She may rest, but she never stops.

She also trains with the masters. I currently have two coaches, and they are the best thing that happens to me. One of them is a very tough coach, and she doesn't let me play small. Working with her is why you are reading this today. The other, slightly gentler in nature coach helps me unwind the information of my very non-linear processes, dreams, metaphors and Four Voices. I hope you decide to work with a coach that fits you. That coach may even be me—if it's a fit for us to work together, I would be delighted. Of course, my contact information can be found at the end of this book.

When Rian feels rattled by the world and about to distract, she is able to immediately resource by grounding and setting up her strong boundary. This connection to earth strength and present time enables her to focus her energies and begin to explore what she needs in the moment to take care of herself.

She can determine which chakra she may need to

access in order to discover the root of the disturbance. Is this a root chakra survival issue or is she bumping up against a self-confidence solar plexus chakra discomfort? She can use the chakra-related questions to establish her next course of action.

Rian may need to use her Mind Voice to question thoughts or judgments causing her to feel off balance. She may want to just sit quietly and focus on her breath to calm her mind. Maybe a walk in nature will help to sort out jumbled thinking. She knows she has options and that she is better off if she uses them.

When she feels pain or an unusual sensation in her body, Rian knows that a conversation with her Body Voice is probably in order. She may make her way to her yoga mat or just hold the body part that is hurting. She waits and the body answers in a memory, color, or image that helps her to decipher how her body wants her to take care.

Now that Rian is friends with her Heart Voice—emotions are welcomed and treated more like guests than strangers. Certainly, it was not easy in the beginning (it isn't for any of us) and, as Rian works closely with me, she becomes more emotionally fluent. She remembers the questions for each feeling. It's a powerful practice to be able to ask your fear, "What action needs to be taken?"

There will always be noise and the storms of life for Rian. She is human. This is life. And as the thunder crashes about her, she hears the call of her Soul Voice like a high, sweet hymn piercing through the veil. This voice is now clear, and when she is faced with challenges, she knows how to get quiet and receive the messages of all her voices. These practices bring in the grace of her Soul.

The elegance of Grounding and Boundaries and the Magic Keys appears when you are able to weave them into one another. It becomes like a favorite song, part of your make-up and deepest nature.

I do believe that sober humans, should we survive the ravages of trauma and addiction, are the lucky ones. We face our demons on a daily basis and are the true bad asses of society. I hope you understand and embrace that knowledge.

I hope you connect with nature and creatures and find magic. Carry that torch into the night. Humanity needs stories of wildness and mystery to combat the paving-over of our boldness and animal natures. We are made of stars and stardust, moonlight and the clay of the earth.

I hope you will yoga your great big heart out, as it will connect your body with your heart, mind, and soul in ways that are also a mystery.

I hope you read and study and play with all the resources I have referenced in this book. The complete list can be found in the reference section. These books and programs are the ones I wished I had known about in my early sobriety. They may have given me much understanding and may have been a light when all lights seemed to go out.

I hope this book is also that light for you.

I hope you learn healthy boundaries to bring you much safety and that you learn what you truly like and what you truly want. I hope you become so flexible that when those wants change, you honor those changes. I hope you become so graceful at surrender that life flows through you and takes you on adventure after adventure that you couldn't even have imagined.

I hope I get the honor and delight of witnessing and being a part of these grand adventures of yours. Please feel free to be in touch.

Every wise adventurer brings a guide.

Adventurer's Knapsack

The following is a list of the things that I take on all of my adventures, both daily and on longer journeys.

dōTERRA essential oils and supplements—as a doctor, I have the opportunity to be exposed to many wonderful products. My life began to expand when I started using these oils, and I wish I'd had them in early sobriety. I can help you decide which oils to use and where to start. I highly recommend this particular brand, as **dōTERRA** sets the industry standard for purity, safety, your health, and the health of the planet.

Proper nutrition and hydration

Regular exercise (that you enjoy!)

Regular time spent outdoors

Proper sleep

Loads of reading and research into subjects that interest you (see recommended reading list)

Lots of hugs and human interaction

But also quality time spent in solitude

YOGA

Meditation

Body-centered therapy and coaching

Play, dance, laugh

Feel your emotions

Spend time with animals

Reach out, help others

Find work that feeds your soul

References

INTRODUCTION

Tommy Rosen—Vinyasa flow and kundalini yoga teacher—a leading authority on addiction and recovery with twenty years of experience helping people overcome addictions of every kind—founder of the Recovery 2.0 online conference and author of *Recovery 2.0: Move Beyond Addiction and Upgrade Your Life*

Noah Levine—American Buddhist teacher and the author of *Dharma Punx: A Memoir* (2004), *Against the Stream: A Buddhist Manual for Spiritual Revolutionaries* (2007), *The Heart of the Revolution: The Buddha's Radical Teachings on Forgiveness, Compassion, and Kindness* (2011), and *Refuge Recovery: A Buddhist Path to Recovering from Addiction* (2014)

Dr. Gabor Maté—renowned addiction expert who calls for a compassionate approach toward addiction, whether in ourselves or in others—believes the source of addiction to be found not in genes but in the early childhood environment—author of *In the Realm of Hungry Ghosts*, which draws on cutting-edge science and real-life stories to show how all addictions originate in trauma and emotional loss

Johann Hari—Swiss-British writer and journalist—author of *Chasing the Scream: The First and Last Days of the War on Drugs*

CHAPTER ONE

Meadow DeVor—Master-certified coach, spiritual teacher, yogi, and Rowdy who has devoted her practice to helping women live healthier, more meaningful lives—author of *The Tao of Rowdy*, *The Tao of Rowdy Workbook*, and *Money Love: A Guide to Changing the Way You Think about Money*—credit for "The Four Voices" goes to Meadow and is used with permission.

CHAPTER TWO

Bessel van der Kolk—Boston-based psychiatrist noted for his research in the area of post-traumatic stress since the 1970s—focuses on the interaction of attachment, neurobiology, and developmental aspects of trauma's effects on people—author of *The Body Keeps the Score*.

CHAPTER THREE

Credit for all references and questions related to each chakra goes to **Anodea Judith**, author of *Eastern Body, Western Mind*

CHAPTER FOUR

Michael Singer, author of *The Untethered Soul*—Thought Work by **Byron Katie**

CHAPTER FIVE

Louise Hay, author of *You Can Heal Your Life*—**Dr.**

John E. Sarno, author of *Healing Back Pain: The Mind-Body Connection*—all references and body/chakra-related questions compiled from and credit given to **Anodea Judith**, author of *Eastern Body, Western Mind*

CHAPTER SIX

All questions related to each emotion complied from and credited to **Karla McLaren**, author of *The Language of Emotions*—**Jodi Krahn**,Somatic Psychotherapist ,Life Coach, Inquiry Yoga Teacher and founder of GatherHer

CHAPTER SEVEN

Anam Cara: A Book of Celtic Wisdom by **John O'Donohue**—*The Language of Emotions* by **Karla McLaren**—*The Yamas and Niyamas: Yoga's Ethical Principles* by **Deborah Adele**

CHAPTER EIGHT

Dave Ramsey of Financial Peace University—**Meadow DeVor**, author of *Money Love*—**Angela Lauria** of The Author Incubator

CHAPTER NINE

Dr. Gabor Maté and **Bessel van der Kolk** (see reference to the introduction)

CHAPTER TEN

A Course in Miracles by **Dr. Helen Schucman—** *Chasing the Scream* by **Johann Hari—***Anam Cara* by **John O'Donohue**

CHAPTER ELEVEN

The Lord of the Rings by **J.R.R. Tolkien**

Recommended Reading

I don't know what I would do without books in my life. The following is a list of books that are close to my heart and have shone much light on my path.

The Hobbit and *The Lord of the Rings Trilogy* by J.R.R. Tolkien

Anam Cara: A Book of Celtic Wisdom by John O'Donohue

Recovery 2.0: Move Beyond Addiction and Upgrade Your Life by Tommy Rosen

Chasing the Scream: The First and Last Days of the War on Drugs by Johann Hari

The Body Keeps the Score: Brain, Mind and Body in the Healing of Trauma by Bessel Van Der Kolk, M.D.

Healing Back Pain: The Mind-Body Connection by John E. Sarno, M.D.

The Surrender Experiment and *The Untethered Soul* by Michael Singer

The Language of Emotions by Karla McLaren

Eastern Body, Western Mind: Psychology and the Chakra System as a Path to the Self by Anodea Judith

You Can Heal Your Life by Louise Hay

The Yamas and Niyamas: Exploring Yoga's Ethical Practice by Deborah Adele

Restorative Yoga for Life by Gail Boorstein Grossman, E-RYT, 500, CYRT

Emotions and Essential Oils: The Reference Guide published by Enlighten

Acknowledgements

I had no idea I was going to write a book. I'd thought about it and maybe even started a book or two way in the distant past. Because I'm not an epic fantasy novel writer, I figured that ship had sailed long ago.

Enter Angela Lauria, her fantastic staff, and the Difference Process. I submitted an application as a game (I thought it would prove that I *couldn't* write) and consequently pushed away every single "I can't" story I had about myself to get this book written. Thank you for reminding me over and over to *just love* my people. Thank you for the brilliant, hard path to making a difference and for the enormous growth. I am not the same person who started this journey.

To my family and friends who may or may not have had some serious concerns about my sanity. You trusted me anyway and supported me with great love, excitement, and encouragement. Thank you.

For my dear clients and students who not only teach me every single day about bravery, magic, and courage but also shared their stories so that more people may discover their inner beauty and strength. This work is *not* for the timid.

For Morgan Sandberg and Karen Purcell, you were my only sober friends when I embarked on my sobriety journey, and you saved my life. Bestie, Marcie Walker, thank you for picking up the pieces and for the solid friendship throughout the years—we bring out the best in each other. Shannon Brown, you are a soul friend indeed. Thank for the deep conversations, rituals, and "burny" things.

To my dear, sober, yoga tribe, Doug and Andrea Moore, Karen Lillyman, Cindy Farnes, Charelle Durant, and Heather Rocke, who wanderlusted with me in 2016. Being a part of your sobriety, growth, and expansion is a gracious gift. You helped me become consistent with my yoga practice and discover Tommy Rosen (Recovery 2.0), which led me to listen to Meadow DeVor and realize in an instant that I *had* to work with her.

Meadow, your training and your work changed my life dramatically, again. You gave me all the things to create boundaries and understand what the heck had transpired in my life. Not only that—you also gave me the gift of understanding my problems and the coolest ways to work them out. These Magical Keys are shared in this book to support more people out of addiction of any kind. Thank you for teaching me to become a truth teller even when it's hard and to live an authentic life.

My Yoga Church, soul sisters, and master coaches, I could not have done this without you. I'm in so much gratitude for your friendship, inspiration, and strength.

Jodi Krahn and Angela Lauria, my "iron fist in a velvet glove" coaches, thank you for calling me on my crap and encouraging me to play *huge*.

My fellow authors in The Difference Process, wow! You're vulnerability and striving for excellence gave me more courage and inspiration than you may have realized.

Ally Nathaniel and AN Better Publishing, thank you for your guidance and holding my hand throughout the publishing process.

Thank you to Chelsea Walsh for the fantastic cover and author photos and much gratitude as well goes to Jon Criss for designing a beautiful Chakra image.

For my community (with too many members to name—you know who you are), for which I share great love and growth. Thank you for sharing your grace.

Thank you to Great Full Gardens for giving me a place to heal and, ultimately, for unceremoniously kicking me out of the nest. Sometimes the greatest gifts come wrapped in really funny packages.

Dearest Court Jester Little Bug pup, even though you left this realm on September 14, 2015, I know you run with me and guide me on all the trails and trials. I still do not understand why you had to go, but knowing you are still here and part of this story, I'll take it.

For all the pups that I share my life with, thank you for the unwavering love and tail wags. Zoe, you danced your way into my heart and healed my soul.

Finally, to my Soul Voice for guiding me to get sober, face my problems, and use that entire struggle to help others. To my own tenacity for always searching for a better, different adventure and my absolute insistence on communing with nature and all its creatures to nurture and heal. Woman, you are kind of a badass, and I'm pretty happy to have met you.

If I somehow mistakenly left someone out, please forgive me.

Now it's your turn. Live big, embrace your solitude, learn to open more fully to give and receive love, and make a difference.

I bow to all of you and God in gratitude and humility. Namasté.

About the Author

Dr. Layne Linebaugh is a recovering chiropractor, who has been on an adventure of sobriety since February 2013.

She is a "survivor" of trauma, disconnection, and addiction. She is now thriving in the presence, clarity, and connection of a sober life.

Layne has trained and graduated in numerous techniques from those in the field of Chiropractic to NLP and Clinical Hypnotherapy. Her expertise in working with the human body and her love of movement, coupled with personal and spiritual growth, led her to certification in the unique and effective combination of Restorative Yoga and Life (Sobriety) Coaching.

Dr. Linebaugh is the owner and founder of Soul Story Yoga and Coaching. She leads workshops and classes and enjoys a thriving one-on-one practice.

Her own path through great difficulty and problems, before and during sobriety, pushed her to expand her skills as a writer and author so she could help more people gain peace and fulfillment through these unique practices of the mystery of being human.

Layne Linebaugh lives, breathes, and communes with nature in Reno, Nevada. She shares her path with close friends, family, and pup companion, Zoe Sparkle Pants.

Thank You

Thank you for joining me on this adventure. I want you to be able to access your own unique voices as much and as often as possible. In the interest of helping you do so, I have a special gift for you. Just send me an email at <u>DcLayneL@msn.com</u> for a video recording of a restorative yoga sequence that shows you how to match the chakra questions with poses and corresponding areas of the body. This gift is free and I look forward to connecting with you.

Made in the USA
Columbia, SC
12 May 2018